Science&
Language
Links

Science & Language Links

Classroom Implications

Edited by Johanna Scott

HEINEMANN
Portsmouth, NH

Heinemann
A division of Reed Publishing (USA) Inc.
361 Hanover Street Portsmouth, NH 03801-3912

Offices and agents throughout the world

First U.S. printing 1993
Originally published in 1992 by the Australian Reading Association Ltd.

Library of Congress Cataloging–in–Publication Data

Science and language links : classroom implications / edited by
Johanna Scott
  p. cm.
 Includes bibliographical references.
 ISBN 0–435–08338–4 (alk. paper)
 1. Science —Study and teaching (Elementary)—Australia.
 2. Language arts (Elementary)—Australia. I. Scott, Johanna.
LB1585.5.A8S37 1993
372.3'5044'0994—dc20   92—44250
                            CIP

Printed in the United States of America on acid free paper
03 02 01 00 VP 5 6 7 8 9

Acknowledgements

I started this book with the naive notion that editing a book would be easier and quicker than writing one. After soliciting chapters, seeking readers' comments, suggesting reworkings (often several times) and rejecting contributions, I now know that this is not the case. I wish to thank the people who supported me when difficult decisions were made and when self-doubt struck. I have gained tremendously in both professional and personal ways by shaping and editing this book.

I would like to thank the many people who have supported and assisted me. Firstly I am indebted to the authors, David Keystone, Lyn Turner, Jenny Feely, Lesley Wing Jan, Nea Stewart-Dore, Beverly Derewianka and Jo Coffey, a talented group of professionals who have so clearly put forward their views and responded to each other's work. I also thank Denise Ryan, Diane Snowball, Marie Emmitt, Russell Tytler, Kathy Paige and Kay Moulton-Graham for their assistance. Lisa Berryman has been a wonderful copy-editor. My colleagues at Deakin University were particularly supportive and, of course, thank you to Ian and Andrew Scott who spent a great deal of time entertaining each other.

CONTENTS

Introduction ix

Part 1   **Science and Talking** 1

Chapter 1   Reflective Questions: David Keystone 3

Chapter 2   Second Language Science: Lyn Turner 19

Part 2   **Science and Writing** 25

Chapter 3   Writing in Science: Jenny Feely 27

Chapter 4   Ways of Writing Science: Lesley Wing Jan 39

Part 3   **Science and Reading** 53

Chapter 5   Ways of Reading Science: Nea Stewart-Dore 55

Chapter 6   Reading Secondary Science Textbooks: Beverly Derewianka 67

Chapter 7   Learning Science from Books: Jo Coffey 81

About the Authors 89

INTRODUCTION

We know that children naturally attempt to make sense of their world and that language plays a key role in their learning. The roles that language plays in science learning, the ways that science can be used to develop children's language, and how increased knowledge of language goes hand in hand with the development of scientific ideas provide the key focus for this book.

Successful classrooms provide children with a range of science activities to investigate. Children pull apart toys to see how they work and then use this information to make their own toys. They collect and examine plants and insects and become fascinated by how the slater curls up when touched, how the snail safely negotiates a knife blade, with the structure of different leaves and the relationship between the animals and their habitats. While investigating, children have many opportunities to reconstruct their experiences: to use language to make sense of what might otherwise be chaotic impressions. Children are encouraged to talk about what they observe and try to explain it. They write down the things that magnets attract, draw pictures of the structures of leaves, make predictions about the result of placing a knife, blade up, in with the snails, and keep tallies of the number of times different balls bounce. The distances a toy truck travels after leaving an increasingly inclined ramp is recorded, then graphed so that children can draw conclusions about the relationship between slope and distance.

Children want to find out about the world around them and in the process observe, predict, explain, question and devise activities through talking, writing and reading to construct their own meanings. As teachers, we need to understand how language supports science and how we can use science to develop children's language.

In this book, we examine the learning and teaching links between science and language. This introduction provides an overview by focusing on what we mean by learning science, what we mean by learning language, using language to learn science and using science to learn language. The rest of the book is divided into three parts: Science and Talking, Science and Writing and Science and Reading.

WHAT DO WE MEAN BY LEARNING SCIENCE?

If we look at science as being all that contributes to helping children to understand the world around them, then the knowledge that children may find out could include the following:

- the characteristics of living and non-living things and how they can be used to classify and label;
- how certain things behave or work to interact with other things;
- what is needed to change something from one position, state or form to another. (Harlen, 1990).

Freyberg and Osborne (1985) provide us with a useful perspective on the processes children use to learn science when they state that we are teaching science when we help children:

- to investigate things and explore ideas;
- to ask useful and productive questions;
- to seek and develop explanations that are sensible and useful to them, with respect to the natural and technological worlds that they confront daily;
- to broaden their experience of nature and technology;
- to become interested in the explanations of others about how such explanations have been obtained.

The similarities and differences between children's science and the science of scientists are of central importance in the learning and teaching of science. Children come to school with their own meanings for words used in science teaching and their own views of the world which relate to ideas taught in science. These views are strongly held and are often significantly different from those held by scientists. For example, the word 'animal' conjures up pictures of pets or farm animals in the minds of most children. They usually do not include themselves in this category the way biologists do. Children often think that small things float and large things sink, that trees move to make the wind. These and other views seem sensible and coherent to children and they can remain uninfluenced or be influenced in unanticipated ways by science teaching. As teachers, we need to listen to children's explanations to gain insight into the views they hold so that we can plan appropriate classroom experiences.

WHAT DO WE MEAN BY LEARNING LANGUAGE?

The conditions under which children learn to talk have been well documented. (Cambourne, 1988). Lindfors (1987) describes the processes children use to learn language. 'Children figure out the oral and written language in their environment by using powerful processing abilities, hypothesising, testing, confirming, disconfirming and revising underlying rules for meaning expression relations.' (Lindfors, 1987). These processing abilities are similar to the ones children use to learn science.

As they use language in varying social and physical contexts, children come to know more about the language itself. They realise the language that is appropriate to specific social settings or that is in books and texts around the home and school. In the same way, they also come to know about the language of science. Philip is a 7-year-old who turned his room into a museum one wet weekend.

PHILIP'S LABELS.

Philip ordered the physical world as he had noticed it in books and during his visits to the museum. His systematic labelling of the types of fish, with a name and a description of each, gives us information about Philip's knowledge of the language of science and of how science uses language to organise the world.

USING LANGUAGE TO LEARN SCIENCE

Language is closely bound to science, and indeed, everything we do. Emmitt and Pollock (1991) describe language as a pane of glass through which we can view our thinking. Looked at in this way, it appears obvious that language is the servant of science, a tool to help children make sense of their world. A greater grasp of language, however, increases our flexibility and ability to construct and reconstruct meanings. So it is important that as children learn science through language, they learn about language. This book is based on the belief that children are active learners, that they construct their own views which should be supported by school. A circuit was described by children as 'the path of an electric current' before they started investigations using batteries, wires and bulbs. Children could not elaborate on this dictionary definition: they did not have the knowledge to match the words. During the course of the unit, children had the opportunity to play with appropriate equipment, hypothesise about what would happen, to try it out, to experiment. They also collected words that started in the same way as 'circuit'. During this time, children constructed their own frames of knowledge which were refined and revised as their investigations progressed. By the end of their investigations, children were able to demonstrate various working circuits and explain the complexities of what was happening and why. 'A circuit is wires all joined together in a sort of a circle. Circuits make many things work. You can make a torch if you join wires, some batteries and a globe. Electricity from the batteries runs through the wires and makes the globe light up. If the light goes out then you have broken the circuit.'

Their teacher had provided the children with opportunities and had questioned, used appropriate vocabulary and encouraged them to talk as they explored to elaborate on their understandings and rework their frames of knowledge to clarify their understandings. The reframing of their concepts ran parallel to their refining of scientific language.

USING SCIENCE TO LEARN LANGUAGE

The specific nature of scientific language can sometimes confuse children because they are familiar with the words in another, everyday context. Take as an example the word, 'conductor'. Children know a conductor as someone who collects money on a bus or tram, or as someone who leads a group of musicians, choral or orchestral. In each case, the conductor is a person. When we look at 'conductor' in science terms, it is a thing, something that allows electricity, heat or sound to pass through it.

As well as learning about the language of science, the language children use during science investigations and learning varies according to its purpose. It is our role to assist children to learn about the language they need as they use it to learn science.

References

Cambourne, B. (1988), *The Whole Story*, Ashton Scholastic, NSW.

Emmitt, M. and Pollock, J. (1991), *Language and Learning*, OUP, Melbourne.

Freyberg, P. and Osborne, R. (1985), 'Assumptions about Teaching and Learning' in *Learning in Science: The Implications of Children's Science*, Heinemann, Portsmouth, NH.

Harlen, W. and Jelly, S. (1990), *Developing Science in the Primary Classroom*, Heinemann, Portsmouth, NH.

Lindfors, J.W. (1987), *Children's Language and Learning*, 2nd. ed. Prentice Hall, New York.

We spend a great deal of time controlling children, asking them questions to which we know the right answer. If we are to engage children in their own learning, we must provide them with opportunities to talk with one another, as well as with teachers and relevant others.

This thought often challenges accepted ideas, enabling, even forcing, children to reorganise their thoughts.

Two functions of talk, exploratory and presentational, are identified by Barnes (1988). Exploratory talk is where children collaborate and talk, often in a hesitant manner, to consider and arrange their ideas. Presentational talk is where children report on what they have discovered. It has an important evaluative function. If, however, we want children to construct their own meanings, then we need to place a greater emphasis on exploratory talk.

As they engage in exploratory talk during their investigations, children collaborate to build up joint hypotheses and add new ideas to what has gone before. They explore interrelationships and rearrange information to determine its significance.

In this section of the book, David Keystone writes of the positive role he plays in the talk that accompanies science investigations about mirrors in his classroom. He listens to children, makes suggestions, questions the children and encourages them to ask questions of themselves and one another.

Lyn Turner shows us how science activities are a wonderful vehicle for learning another language, whether that be English or a community language.

References

Barnes, D. (1988), 'Oral Language and Learning' in Hynds, S. and Rubin, D. (eds). *Perspectives on Talk and Learning*, NCTE, Urbana, Illinois.

David Keystone

....

INTRODUCTION

This is a case study of significant 'snapshots' of a science unit. These snapshots offer some insights into the way learning is influenced by children and teacher discourse, particularly in the area of questioning and answering.

The unit on Mirrors was planned and implemented in a multi-age class of twenty-nine 10- to 12-year-old children. The transcripted dialogue, the learning contexts and the evaluative comments reveal the importance placed on questioning and the way this influences and promotes thinking.

Osborne and Freyberg (1985) emphasise that the teacher and the children need to share common goals and purpose in class activity. The teacher's role becomes that of encourager, experimenter, guide, challenger and innovator. It is this teacher role that is explored in this study.

Starting and working with children's perceptions and building upon their past experiences makes learning enjoyable, goals achievable and acknowledges the learners as active participants in their own learning.

The teaching task then becomes that of designing and carrying out activities that best reflect the children's interests and ideas, of allowing them to raise their own questions, plan and carry out their own investigations and finally, of making sure that children draw conclusions based on sound evidence related to their personal experiences, either inside or outside the classroom.

THE SPARK: INITIATING THE TOPIC

A group of children were discussing and reading a novel. One girl shielded her eyes from the glare of our classroom's tinted windows. She complained that the glare was too strong for her to sit in her original position. She moved. She and I each commented on light reflecting from various surfaces and how this can annoy and aggravate.

The school had produced numerous Science Unit boxes. These boxes are collections of materials and equipment sufficient for a teacher to use with a class of thirty children. Children's books and teacher references are also included. The 'Mirrors and Magnifiers' unit box had recently been put together, and I had planned to use it. This experience with reflecting light was coincidental but most fortuitous in terms of my planning.

TEACHER PREPARATION FOR THE UNIT

I collected the unit box entitled 'Mirrors and Magnifiers' from the school's science resource room; it consisted of:

A sturdy plastic box	6 concave mirros	a kaleidoscope (commercially made)
3 small prisms	6 convex mirrors	10 workcards

I left the box in the room for one week and watched for some curiosity. I informed the children that the mirrors were for our science investigations the following week. I browsed through the school library and found suitable books on the topic of mirrors. For example, *Mirrors and Magnifiers* by Bennett, *David Suzuki asks — Did you know about light and sight?* by Suzuki and Cook, *Investigating Light*, The Young Scientist Series, *Light Fantastic* by Watson, *Light Lenses and Colour* by Fice and Simkiss, *Light Mirrors and Lenses*, Ladybird Junior Science, *Light and Colour*, MacDonald First Library, *Exploring Light and Colour* by Neal, *The Science Book* by Stein and *Light — Read About Science 3* by Stephenson.

I set some objectives and learning outcomes related to science and language processes as well as content; they included:

- To increase children's knowledge about mirrors: mirrors are shiny surfaces and reflect light; some materials are better reflectors than others.

- To extend and widen children's vocabulary associated with light, mirrors and reflection.

- To have children construct something out of mirrors by following oral and written instructions, thereby examining the nature and purpose of instructional writing.

- For children to practise and improve their ability to locate, make sense of and use information from non-fiction texts and illustrations.

Setting the scene is an important consideration. Arranging a display of relevant objects, books and posters in the classroom, and encouraging children to touch them, talk about them and to bring things of their own are useful strategies in stimulating and initiating interest.

ENTRY POINT: ENGAGING THE LEARNERS

I asked the children to respond to the question 'How can I use a mirror?' by recording a list of uses. The children completed the task individually. Several of them read their lists to the class. Comments were invited and necessary changes or additions were made.

This activity revealed and identified the prior knowledge and experience that children bring to the classroom. It acknowledges and gives credence to the children's abilities and ideas. From this initial activity they see that they have important contributions to make to their own learning. The collective knowledge of the class group is also revealed and may trigger off new and different thoughts and ideas.

JODIE'S LIST OF USES FOR A MIRROR.

FIRMING THE ENGAGEMENT THROUGH PLAY

I gave each child a pair of mirrors. I asked them to find out as much as they could by doing [handwritten: Opportunity for talk and exploration] things with their mirrors. Some looked at their faces. Others put the mirrors to either side of their faces and then looked into either mirror. I was called upon to verify and acknowledge numerous phenomena and discoveries.

The children's thinking can be stimulated and their ideas and abilities revealed and demonstrated to the teacher, whose role is that of encourager and organiser. From the outset children need time to play and to investigate. This stage should not be rushed, nor should it be overly structured by the teacher. At this stage there is no 'right answer', and the teacher's role is that of encourager. The children invent, experiment, imitate and demonstrate. The teacher joins in, roves, comments, observes and asks questions of individuals and groups of individuals.

EMILY AND BELINDA EXPERIMENT WITH SMALL MIRRORS.

Observations of Children Engaged in Play

- Pairs of children placed their mirrors standing up on the ground to make a box shape. They placed objects within the box and observed and counted.

- One child angled the mirrors and reflected one on to another. He claimed he was making a periscope.

- One child walked backwards looking for obstacles in both mirrors held in front of her.

- One child stood his mirrors together in a V-shape and placed a stone in between and observed and commented on what he saw.

- One child looked inside her mouth at her teeth and tongue.

- One child reflected the sun on another classroom's windows.

Throughout the session the children talked about things reflecting, bouncing, multiplying. I acknowledged and commented with:

'That's a good idea. What do you think of that...?'

'What do you think would happen if you put two stones in between the mirrors?'

'How many times are you repeated in the mirror? Is it the same number for each side?'

'I wonder what's happening?'

'What have you found out so far?'

'Could you make a mirror signal to a friend by reflecting the sun's light?'

'That sounds like fun. Show me how you did it.'

key questions

I asked the children to commence writing a daily diary to document and enhance their learning. The following questions acted as a guide:

What did I do?

With whom did I work?

What did I learn?

Did I enjoy learning?

What am I good at?

Diary of Wonderful Mirrors

19·6·91 — John. H.

Today our class created a rainbow by using a mirror and a piece of card board. The water reflected off the mirror which beamed on to the card board It worked perfectly. I worked with Scott Williams. I learned how to make a rainbow with only a piece of card and a mirror and some water. I enjoyed learning very much, especially when the colors came up.

AN ENTRY FROM JOHN'S DIARY.

PROMOTING QUESTIONS AND QUESTIONING

Prior to the next session I set up a book display. I left some workcards about mirrors near the book display. I distributed some instructions from a book on making things using mirrors. I said that I would like everybody to read a book, an instruction sheet or card. I said that I would like each person to take notes or write questions based on their reading. I gave examples:

- Circle an experiment you like.

- Write a question.

- Write an experiment from a book.

After fifteen minutes I asked the class to tell me any questions they had about mirrors: for example, things that puzzle them or things they would like to find out about. I recorded these questions on paper strips that were displayed as a reference focus for the remainder of the unit. For example:

List of Questions Posed by Children

1. How do you make a rainbow with a mirror?

2. How does a mirror make an image different?

3. Who invented the first mirror?

4. Why is it that when I look into a mirror and move my left arm it looks as though my right arm is moving?

5. When was the first mirror made?

6. What sort of glass is a mirror made out of?

7. How does a mirror show your face in such detail?

8. What is a photon?

9. How does the sun give energy?

10. How are mirrors made?

11. When you put a pencil in a glass why does it look bent?

12. How can you see a letter (of the alphabet) back to front?

13. How do some mirrors make you look bigger or smaller than you really are?

14. How many different mazes can you make with a mirror?

15. How does the sun reflect off the mirror through the glass of water to make a rainbow?

16. How is a rainbow made?

17. How do mirrors reflect?

18. What are mirrors made of?

19. How does one mirror send its rays to another mirror?

20. How could you use a mirror in the bush to attract someone?

21. Why do mirrors stick together when they are rubbed?

22. Can mirrors be used to make heat?

23. In a periscope, how do mirrors make you see the image you are looking at?

24. How does the sun shine on one side of the mirror and reflect on the other?

25. How do you send messages to another person using mirrors?

26. Is the glass used to make mirrors different from the glass used to make windows?

27. What is a mirrorball?

28. How do you see yourself in the mirror?

29. Why is a kaleidoscope round on the outside and in parts on the inside?

30. How does a kaleidoscope work?

31. Why are the classroom windows mirrors on the outside?

32. Why is everybody upside down when I hold the mirror above my eyes?

33. Why is the back of the mirror, the painted side, not as smooth as the glass side?

34. How fast does light travel?

Providing the children with an opportunity to ask questions about a topic stimulates others in the class to think about aspects of the topic that they may not have considered. The questions posed by some children challenge others to broaden their ideas about the topic. If some of the children struggle with the notion of asking a question, the teacher can provide a sound role model by also asking and contributing a question. Accepting and acknowledging children's questions in this way affirms the role they can play in their own learning. It also serves to increase questioning behaviour.

POSING QUESTIONS

Harlen (1989) states, 'the ability to convert general possibilities into action questions for children to tackle is probably the most important skill in planning science work'. The intention is to produce and, where appropriate, select questions that lead the children to observe things not noticed before and to help them build on their existing ideas. Learning and commitment to the task improves when children have a say in the directions and focus of their investigations.

Should such investigative activity be unfamiliar to a group, children reporting their intended areas of study and foci to the class act as models. The discourse shows how ideas and, more specifically, questions, can be shared and built upon by other class members.

The teacher's role is that of facilitating the exchange between the presenter and audience. There is a genuine purpose in the children sharing their reports with others.

I asked the class to write things under the following headings, either individually or in small groups.

- What I want to know or do.
- How I will find out.
- What I will need.

Exploring Mirrors

What I want to know or do!	How I will find out!	What I will need!
I want to know secret code	I will find out by exploring a way to show me.	Mirror, papper, pen
Write to a mirror making company	By writing to them.	envelope, pen, stamps
I want to make a periscope	By experimenting	Milk cartons, tape, mirrors
Mirror Maze	I will find out by experimenting	Mirror, papper, pen
Images	Looking into Mirrors and pikung up Images that are diffent	mirror

ERIC'S COMPLETED PROJECT SHEET.

I prompted them to use:
- Their reading to help them.
- The questions displayed around the room.

- Their early free play session.

- Other people's ideas.

- Their imagination and sense of fun.

- The Mirrors class word list on the display board.

I asked a child to report to the class about her project sheet.

Belinda: I will write to a mirror factory.

Teacher: What do you want to find out?

Belinda: Questions like... What kind of glass are mirrors made of? What was the first mirror made from?

Teacher: Are there any questions or comments about Belinda's task?

PAUSE

Teacher: Has anyone got any questions they would like Belinda to ask?

Integration Aid: What sort of paint do they use on the back of the glass?

Belinda: Oh... yes... and... um, what materials and tools do you need to make a mirror?

Matthew: How a mirror is made?

CHALLENGING AND CHECKING: TELLING A STORY ABOUT RAINBOWS

I talked with six children about rainbows. The day before I demonstrated a spectrum on a piece of white cardboard. I angled the mirror and reflected the sun's rays through the water in a tub. It produced a spectrum. I wanted to know what the children understood about rainbows, such as:

- Where is the sun in relation to you when observing a rainbow?

- How and when does a rainbow appear?

- How can we check this out?

I asked the children to start by telling me the story of how a rainbow appears.

Daniel: I think it's behind you and sort of on the side of you.

Teacher: Why do you think that?

Daniel: Well, it's just on an angle, sort of, so... it just reflects to a rainbow.

Jodie: It's also that…I don't know why…but just if you're looking at a rainbow straight on…the sun looks like it's on the side…say, it's on the left-hand or the right-hand side more than in the centre.

There then ensued a three-minute discussion. After this, the following discourse occurred:

Michael: I think the sun comes down…right. And all the droplets they all form like reflection of a mirror and you know like we did with the water. With water you can see yourself. We did it with the mirror and the water…but the sun does it with only the water. And it just reflects. So the sun would have to be behind it to reflect under the rain to reflect the rainbow.

Teacher: Okay. When you're standing looking at a rainbow where do you think the sun is in relation to you?

Michael: If I'm looking at it it'd be to the left-hand side up there at the back of the rainbow.

Teacher: How could we check this out?

Bianca: On a rainy day…and it's sunny…and then we have a sun shower.
After the sun shower the rainbow will come. I can see it just by looking at it.

Troy: What about looking it up in a book…encyclopaedia…dictionary…or a book about light.

Two days later.

Taryn: I found this book over there and it says (reading to the teacher) 'When you look at a rainbow the sun is behind you' and see there's a picture…

Some weeks later, following the sighting of a rainbow phenomenon, various children excitedly reported that the sun was behind them as they were facing the rainbow.

The teacher's questions can challenge and stimulate the children's thinking. The discourse shows the children trying to clarify, describe and explain a rainbow. They endeavour to review their past experience in the light of such diverse opinion. Being told the right answer may do little to modify their earlier views. They may merely carry two perspectives, the teacher's and their own, whereby they apply the first in school and the second outside school.

The personal observations, experience and research may contribute significantly towards reaching an accurate view. This challenge is quite able to be investigated simply through careful observation at an appropriate time and place, including sightings made out of schooltime. These observations should be acknowledged, supported and encouraged.

Initially the children expressed quite diverse and strong views about the relative position of the sun to a viewer observing a rainbow. Some children may explain the appearance of a rainbow phenomenon in the same way as they attempted to explain the earlier experiment of making a spectrum. A teacher's attempts at creating simulations of this kind need to be examined for their worth in assisting with the investigation. Simulating a spectrum in the manner described needs to be thought through and understood in order to be considered useful in describing and explaining a rainbow phenomenon. In this specific example, the personal reporting by the children of their observations is significant in verifying other sources of information.

DEALING WITH QUESTIONS: USING HANDS-ON EXPERIMENTS AND CHILDREN DEMONSTRATING

The teacher's role is one of encouraging. Encouraging those who were puzzling over a phenomenon to make sense of it and supporting the young expert who attempted to describe and explain. Question and statement prompts from the teacher maintain the children's interest and curiosity in the investigation.

Malcolm and Scott agreed to investigate the question of 'How does a kaleidoscope work?' They have the commercially made kaleidoscope from the unit box. They looked through the tube and pointed it in the direction of the class lights.

Malcolm: I reckon there might be two mirrors.

Scott: I think there's five.

Teacher: Why do you think there's more than two?

Scott: Because if there were two it would double the image. If there were four it would double it again...

Teacher: How do you think the mirrors are placed in the kaleidoscope?

PAUSE

Teacher: If you could cut this open and see inside, tell me the things you think you would find in it?

Malcolm: A mirror.

Teacher: Whereabouts?

Malcolm: In the lens bit...here.

I asked the pair to look at the peephole of the kaleidoscope. They observed the bottom part of the V-shape formation of the mirrors inside the kaleidoscope.

Teacher: Try putting your mirrors in that position.

They did so.

Scott: The mirrors are on an angle so you can see through them. The angle...the way it shows...it's like a triangular angle.

Teacher: Have you seen how a kaleidoscope is made, say, in a book?

Kate: I've made one...you get three mirrors...three long ones...

Teacher: These people think that they can see two there.

Kate: There's two there and then there's one up on top that goes like that (demonstrating).

Malcolm: Oh...now I get it...

Kate: If you look in there you can see a triangle (holding the kaleidoscope and handing it to Malcolm). See, it's a triangle of mirrors...and the mirrors go from side to side to make more patterns...and you join the three mirrors in a triangular shape like that... and then you put some beads in there...and the mirrors reflect the beads...and the mirror will go back to the mirror and the mirror goes back to the mirror and the mirror goes back to the mirror, so there will be millions of beads in there...but you've only got a few in there.

Teacher: Show them how they can make a kaleidoscope using mirrors.

Kate used three mirrors and masking tape. She demonstrated how to make a kaleidoscope. Two other children approached the demonstration. Kate repeated her explanation of the way a kaleidoscope works.

Two days later Scott wrote an answer to the question, 'How does a kaleidoscope work?'

The three mirrors that are inside, are placed in a triangle so when one mirror sees something, it reflects to the other mirrors which makes it look like there are hundreds of what you put in

by Scott Williams

SCOTT'S WRITTEN ANSWER.

So in a short space of time two children's knowledge shifted from being incomplete and vague to a position of basic understanding of how a kaleidoscope is made and works. The children were given time for some independent exploration with a commercially made kaleidoscope. They were challenged to speculate on the inside parts of the kaleidoscope. Following an observation, they were asked to show the way the mirrors are placed.

Kate exemplified the young expert who can be found in many classrooms. Her approach to the group and her inclusion was timely. Her discourse built on the two children's demonstration. Her own demonstration gave meaning to her explanation of the way a kaleidoscope works and, more importantly, it seemed to make sense to the two children who were listening and observing. Through her demonstration and commentary, the expert was able to support the learning of other classmates.

REFLECTING AND REPORTING: MAKING PERISCOPES

JODIE READS THE INSTRUCTIONS AND THEN MAKES A PERISCOPE.

Time spent by children reviewing newly acquired skills provides valuable insights to learning for them as well as the teacher. The dialogue of class investigations shows that primary children are able to reflect critically on their work with rigour and insight. Depending on the types of questions asked by the teacher, children are encouraged to analyse the way in which results are backed up by evidence and to identify ways in which procedures may have been improved. Throughout this running commentary, the children obviously think aloud and mentally revisit the event or significant moments of learning.

Various types of question prompts are used. These include:

Speculative   for example:
> What would you use the periscope for?
> How do you think the periscope works?

Analytical   (recall details, sequences) for example:
> If you made a mistake, what was it?
> When did you realise you'd done the wrong thing?
> What would be the first instruction to the class after they had collected all that was needed for the research?

Evaluative   for example:
> What do you think was the most difficult thing about making a periscope?
> In drawing up a list of instructions for someone else, would you use words, pictures or both?

The questions prompt and promote discussion. Each child's responses reveal much about their perceptions of the best ways to learn. Notions of trial and error, risk taking and sequencing instructions are seen as important by the child.

I interviewed children in front of the class.

Teacher: What would you use the periscope for?

Walid: At the footy if someone's taller than you ... is in front of you just put it up and you can see ...

Sarah demonstrates her periscope.

Sarah: The mirror sees the image ... and then it goes to the mirror ... and reflects to the other mirror and then you see it in that other one ...

Teacher: How many tries did you have at making it?

Sarah: Two

Teacher: What do you think was the most difficult thing about making a periscope?

Sarah: Getting the mirror cuts right . . . in the right direction . . . so you could see . . .

Teacher: What mistake did you make first?

Sarah: I cut mine in the wrong direction so I couldn't see . . .

Teacher: When did you realise you'd done the wrong thing?

Sarah: When I slid the mirror in it was facing the wrong way.

Teacher: How do you think the periscope works?

Jodie: It goes diagonally.

Teacher: What goes diagonally?

Jodie: Because the mirror goes diagonally in the carton it sees an image . . . you look
at the image in one place . . . and . . . because the other mirror is di . . . in the opposite
direction . . . it reflects the image down and you see it.

Teacher: Let's say you had to make some instructions for someone else. Would you use
words, pictures or both?

Jodie: Words and pictures.

Teacher: I'm interested in what you'd draw.

Jodie: I'd draw two milk cartons and then two cuts in the sides and for each stage I'd do a
different drawing.

Teacher: What would be the first instruction after they had collected everything?

Jodie: To measure the windows and the cuts.

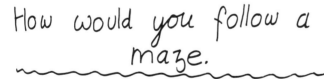

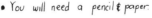

Instructions

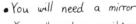

- You will need a mirror
- You will need a pencil & paper.
- Draw up a maze on the paper
- Using the mirror only try, to stay in the lines without going out.
- When your finished you have sealed the test !!!!

DANIEL'S WORKCARD.

EPILOGUE

The children's roles in and responsibilities with their own learning must be acknowledged and valued. As scientists, children follow similar processes to those followed by professional scientists. They set up a problem, carry out some preliminary exploration and investigate. Genuine opportunities for allowing and encouraging questioning helps and supports children learning science.

As children endeavour to articulate their intuitions, beliefs and understandings, teacher and peer intervention through talk influences and shapes learning. This interaction opens the children's minds to further possible explanations and investigations and encourages the children to consider alternative ways of communicating their findings.

The approaches and strategies used and revealed through this case study demonstrate a structure for learning in which anything can and does occur: where language is intimately meshed with understandings and ideas of science; where questioning and questions from the teacher prompt children to think; where children pose questions; where children change their ideas as a direct result of talk and demonstration; where language tasks are authentic and genuine and where questioning and questions are promoted, valued and acknowledged.

References

Harlen W. and Jelly, S. (1990), *Developing Science in the Primary Classroom*, Heinemann, Portsmouth, NH.
Ministry of Education, Victoria (1987), *The Science Framework: P–10*, Melbourne.
Ministry of Education, Victoria (1988), *The Technology Framework: P–10*, Melbourne.
Osborne, R. and Freyberg, P. (1985), *Learning in Science: The implications of children's science*, Heinemann, Portsmouth, NH.

References Used by Children

Bennett, N. (1990), *Mirrors and Magnifiers*, Macmillan, Melbourne.
Fice, R.H.C., and Simkiss, I.M. (1973), *Light Lenses and Colour*, Arnold.
Ladybird Junior Science (1962), *Light Mirrors and Lenses*.
MacDonald First Library (1991), *Light and Colour*, MacDonald, London.
Neal, C. (1965), *Exploring Light and Colour*, Odhams Books.
Stein, S. (1980), *The Science Book*, Workman, New York.
Stephenson, G. (1964), *Light — Read About Science 3*, London.
Suzuki, L. and Cook, P. (1990), *David Suzuki asks — Did you know about light and sight?*, Allen and Unwin, Sydney.
The Young Scientist (1990), *Investigating Light*, World Book Inc., Sydney.
Watson, P. (1983), *Light Fantastic*, Lothrop, New York.

SECOND LANGUAGE SCIENCE

Lyn Turner

Children learning a language other than English (LOTE) or English as a second language (ESL) are supported by the opportunity to engage in science activities. Science activities provide an ideal environment for second language learning as the small group, hands-on, concrete nature of the activities provides the contextual clues to support understanding. Understanding the meaning is essential to language acquisition and ensures that language is acquired at the same time as content learning is explored and extended.

'You *do* know who sank the boat,' read the teacher. Slowly she turned to the following pages of the big book that showed the wet animals walking up the beach towards home. 'Do *you* know who sank the boat?' she said as she looked at the children to invite a response. 'It was the mouse,' a number of children replied as if there was no question about it. 'No, it was all of them,' replied one child. A valuable discussion followed, but few were convinced enough to change their opinion and the question remained unresolved.

'Who thinks it was the mouse?' asked the teacher. Well over half of the children responded. 'Who thinks it was all of them?' Only a couple of children indicated their support for this theory.

A simple graph was made by using the children's photo-pegs (a photo of the child pasted on to the top of a dolly-peg). The teacher wrote two statements: 'The mouse sank the boat' and 'They all sank the boat'. Each child attached their peg close to the appropriate sign. 'How can we find out who is right?' asked the teacher.

The next day the teacher provided a water-tray, a number of stones of appropriate sizes with the animal characters drawn on them and plastic containers to use as boats. Over the next few days small groups of children experimented at the water tray. By the end of the week most of the photo pegs had been attached near the 'They all sank the boat' sign.

The value of reading the book, *Who Sank The Boat?* by Pamela Allen, had been enriched by the opportunity to explore the science concept it presented. (As one animal after another got into the boat the pictures showed how the boat sank lower and lower into the water. Finally the mouse got in and the boat sank.) The book provided a real purpose for the group work that followed and an ideal opportunity for the few children who were learning English as their second language to continue their learning while English was acquired.

The second language learners were able to follow the gist of the story, supported by the wonderful illustrations, the teacher's non-verbal gestures and perhaps comments in their first language from another child. They were able to participate in making the graph and, most importantly, they were able to work in a small co-operative group around the water tray.

Working in a small group with the focus on the task, rather than the language, provides a non-threatening opportunity for the second language learner to listen to the language of the other children and, once confident, to contribute to the conversation. Conversations about 'here and now' things are the building blocks of language learning, as the context supports the understanding of both the speaker and the listener and both conversation partners can adjust their language to ensure greater understanding. Small groups also provide an opportunity for real conversation where meanings are negotiated.

The Prep/Grade One classroom with a few children learning English as a second language provides just one example of how science activities can provide a real purpose and an ideal environment for language learning. All second language learners could benefit from such an approach, including those who attend language centres or schools where all or most of the children are learning English as a second language. It is important that learning continues while English is acquired and that the children are exposed to the language of science in both the spoken and written form.

We must recognise that the medium of instruction is not always English in our schools. The value of maintaining and developing the languages other than English which many children bring to school, or teaching a second language to English-speaking children, has gained greater recognition recently. The children in the aforementioned Prep/Grade One classroom are all learning Italian as a second language. The LOTE teacher uses a whole language approach to Italian and teaches the content of a number of subjects through the medium of Italian.

The hands-on, concrete nature of science makes it an ideal choice as content for learning a LOTE. For example, an Italian science lesson that provided the children with the opportunity to explore the properties of magnets was highly successful, even though the children had limited experience with Italian and the teacher used Italian at all times. The necessary ingredient for language learning was access to meaning through contextual clues and the opportunity to hear and use the language for a real purpose.

The children worked in small groups exploring which objects and surfaces were attracted to the magnets. They recorded their findings on a simple prepared sheet using illustrations. If they knew or asked for the Italian word for various objects, they were encouraged to 'have a go' at labelling. During the sharing time that followed, the LOTE teacher recorded the information the children had discovered on a large sheet of paper. Pictures supported the writing. This provided a model of Italian writing, a chance to hear the Italian word for known objects and a valuable chart to be displayed in the classroom for future reference.

At this early stage of experience with the new language the children use English to ask questions and explain their understandings. Thus, the bilingual LOTE teacher can gauge the level of understanding while using only Italian herself. As with all language learning the children understand much more than they can produce. They are also encouraged when the LOTE teacher enthuses as they include known Italian words and phrases.

The children learned much about magnets through being engaged in 'doing' and finding out for themselves. The use of Italian as the medium of instruction did not inhibit scientific learning. Meaningful exposure to Italian and the opportunity to use the language for a real purpose was an enriching bonus; as was further experience with problem solving, activity-based learning, learning how to learn, co-operative group work and peer tutoring.

Making minestrone soup provided another opportunity to extend scientific knowledge while exposing the children to Italian. Following a visit to the local Italian greengrocer to purchase the ingredients, the children worked in small groups to prepare, cook and eat the delicious soup. Again the LOTE teacher used Italian at all times. She had also made a large recipe chart for reference. This exposed the children to the conventions of recipe writing and gave them a real purpose for reading the Italian words. Illustrations were also added to increase understanding.

The groups checked that they had all the ingredients as the LOTE teacher went through the recipe and read out the ingredients, 'Ingredienti — sedano, cipolle, carote, aglio...'. She then read, 'Metodo. Numero uno. Taglia i vegetali', and the young chefs began to prepare the vegetables. There was a lot of chatter, mostly in English, but the Italian words were used often for the ingredients. As the children worked, some began to sing 'La Canzone del Minestrone' which had been taught during a previous Italian music session.

Using the content of other subject areas ensures that learning continues while the new language is acquired and that valuable time is not taken from other subject areas.

In particular, the investigative small group nature of science activities has considerable potential as a context for language learning and should be explored by ESL, LOTE, science and classroom teachers.

IL MINESTRONE

Ingredienti

sedano
cipolle
carote
aglio
piselli

acqua
sale
pepe
dadi
patate

pomodori
pelati
olio
burro

Metodo

1. Taglia i vegetali

2. Friggi l'olio e il burro in una pentola grande

3. Friggi le cipolle, le carote e l'aglio per 2-3 minuti.

4. Mescola

5. Aggiungi gli altri vegetali

6. Aggiungi l'acqua i dadi, sale, pepe e i pomodori

7. Fai bollire lentamente per un ora e mezzo.

BUON APPETITO!

1½ hours

Reference

Allen, Pamela (1990), Who Sank the Boat? Putnam, New York.

Further Reading

Anthony, J., Conte, D., McKnight, A. and Turner, L. (1991), *Che Fantastico!: Italian Across the Curriculum at Armadale Primary School*, Ministry of Education, Victoria.

Some teachers justify science activities to children by saying, 'We will write it this way because that is what scientists do.' This role-playing at being scientists denies children the knowledge of the real purpose of the tasks in which they engage. A scientist might take notes to observe the relationships between an insect and its habitat during changing weather conditions. The scientist has a hypothesis that needs verifying and so takes notes, draws appropriate diagrams and measures to confirm the hypothesis. Children's writing in science should also be imbedded in reason. They should know the purpose and write in a way that best serves it. Children should be engaged in authentic science activities in the way that scientists are. Their inquiries should start with questions or hypotheses that are clear to the children and are posed by them.

In this section of the book, we move from talk to writing and explore how writing supports science learning and how children can be assisted to develop knowledge about and use of various types of writing. In the words of one 10-year-old child, 'Writing helped me to find out what I knew and what I didn't know.'

In her chapter, Jenny Feely discusses how talk and writing are used in her classroom before, during and after investigations as an integral part of the science learning taking place.

Lesley Wing Jan builds on this and discusses how she explicitly shows children the features and values of written text. This gives the children in her class the freedom to select and use the form of writing that best helps them to come to scientific understandings or present what they have discovered. Not surprisingly, her children choose to write in a wide range of genres, including stories and poems as well as more conventional reports.

WRITING IN SCIENCE

Jenny Feely

All children love to be involved in science experiences both inside and outside the classroom. Children are eager to find out about things, test them, build them, design them, experiment to find out about them and do any number of other tasks that they perceive to be science.

Writing is one of the ways that children learn in science. Recording results and observations enables patterns to be noted and may lead to conclusions being drawn. Drawing diagrams, sketching observations and creating design drawings assists children to communicate their ideas. When children explain what they have seen and why they think this occurs in writing, they are forced to clarify their thoughts and organise these ideas in a way that others can understand.

Children's writing before, during and after science investigations provides a wealth of information to assist teachers in planning and evaluating the development of each child and the effectiveness of the classroom program.

How then do we go about developing suitable writing skills in children?

CAPITALISING ON TALK

As with many other writing experiences, the importance of talk in the science session cannot be overstated. Talking about the investigation is crucial to clarifying thoughts. This talking should be encouraged and developed by the classroom teacher. When the children talk about what they see they clarify their observations. In explaining their ideas they gain a sense of mastery over the ideas they are discussing. Talking also enables questions to be raised. Considering these questions leads to further investigations and the process rolls on. After all, isn't this what science is about? 'Why does that happen?'; 'What will happen if...?'; 'How can we change/control/make that?'; 'What would it be like if (people could fly)?'

Fortunately getting children to talk about science while they are doing it is seldom, if ever, a problem. Children readily talk with others about what they see. Science classes can, therefore, be noisy affairs.

'Look at my roller. It won't work. It won't go up the slope.'

'Your roller won't travel up a slope?'

'I wound it fifty times and it won't go. It just stays in the one spot and unwinds.'

'Will it travel in other places?'

'Yeah. It went on the table.'

'So the roller will travel on the table but not up the three-book slope? Why do you think this is happening?'

'The slope is too big.'

'Will it travel up any slope?'

'I don't know. I'll find out.'

Tammi is learning about the principles of gravity. The roller worked on the flat but will not travel up the table. The greater the gradient the more difficult it is for the roller to work against the pull of gravity.

When Tammi comes to write about her roller and how it worked, she will have a reasonable idea about some of the places the roller was able to travel over and why it couldn't manage to travel on all slopes.

Talking about the 'science' involved during the investigation provides the children with many of the words that they will need to write about the investigation. By modelling new words and ideas generated by the science experience, the teacher provides opportunity for the children to learn about the use of the words in talk. This is often translated to the child's writing. It also provides opportunity to extend the children's knowledge.

'Why does your roller move along the floor?'

'Because I wound it up.'

'What happens when you wind it up?'

'The elastic band gets twisted.'

'Where does the energy to twist the elastic band come from?'

'I don't know.'

'You used your hand to wind it. You used your energy. Your energy went into the elastic band. It was stored there because you held the matchstick.'

'So when I let it go the energy in the elastic band moved the roller.'

This child wrote about their investigation:

> Q. You turn the ice-cream stick which then makes the rubber band twist. You put it on a table and it rolls along as the rubber band unwinds
>
> Q. All the pressure goes into the rubber band which makes the rubber band very tight. When you put the roller down the rubber band un-twists that makes the roller go.

Alert teachers capitalise on this rich talk by listening, reflecting, posing questions and providing new ideas for consideration.

Encouraging talk before the experience can also enable the children to focus their ideas and provides invaluable information for the teacher about the children's current understanding of the area to be studied.

Talking about, then recording, knowledge before beginning an investigation provides a focus: 'This is what we think and this is why we think it.' Recording any questions that arise is also useful. Both can be reviewed as new ideas are formed.

I asked some prep children, 'What is the wind?'

David: All the wind comes on your front and down your back.

Danny: The wind makes you stop. It makes you fly.

Christie: The wind is blowing and the wind is when you blow. That means there's wind in your mouth.

Courtney: The trees make the wind. (How?) When a tree blows that makes all the trees blow. (Thinks.) The trees make the wind by waving their leaves.

I wrote down all of their ideas on a class wall chart. None were mocked or rejected. This record provided a useful reference as we proceeded through a range of experiments and investigations about air. It also provided me with a useful focus for planning appropriate experiences for the children. Experiences that would enable them to find out that air is all around us. That it can push things (including trees). That it can be pushed. That it rises when heated and so on.

After each investigation the children recorded their ideas and I updated our chart as we confirmed some ideas, rejected others and developed and discovered new insights. We talked about air and wrote about it at all stages of the investigation. At the end we were able to record this writing as a group statement:

> *Wind happens because cold air pushes hotter air up and out of the way.*
> *The wind makes the trees move.*

This writing could never have taken place without a huge amount of talking and investigation. After three weeks of diligent work twenty-five children in Prep had developed ideas and understandings that I suspect elude many adults.

Children quickly see the value of recording their ideas for future reference, and this idea is well demonstrated with class charts.

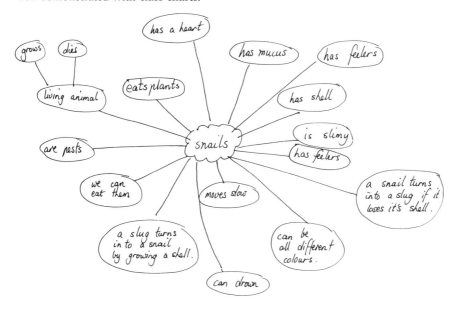

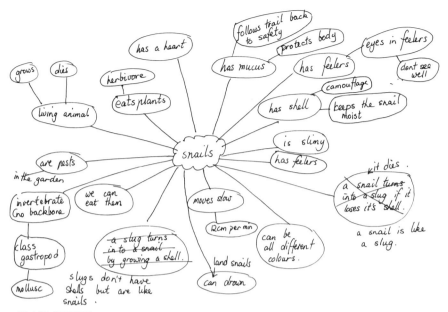

CLASS CHARTS.

By recording the talk that develops throughout the investigation a permanent record can be created. This can be returned to as often as you like to get information and ideas or to challenge as new learning occurs.

As the investigation proceeded we revised and changed the chart often. New things were added: 'Snails are herbivores'. Others were rejected. 'A snail turns into a slug if it loses its shell' became 'slugs don't have shells but are like snails'. The chart was a record of ideas and knowledge and enabled the children to focus on what had been said days before in a way that would otherwise be impossible.

Children will use the chart to support their discussions:

'We found out that snails have thousands of tiny teeth. It says so on the chart.'

'You spell radular like this. It's on the chart.'

Children can also devise their own charts of things known and questions which can be added to and refined as new knowledge is developed.

WRITING BEFORE THE SCIENCE INVESTIGATION

Writing that takes place before children begin a series of investigations can be of great use to the children. This writing can include the collection of information already known or believed by the children, as mentioned. It can also include a record of the purpose of the investigation, the prediction about expected results and the plan of the procedure to be undertaken.

Clarifying the reason for the investigation assists children to focus during the course of the experience. Planning the experience also helps to keep the investigation on track. This can be done as a whole class or in co-operative groups.

> *We are trying to find out what a snail prefers to eat. We are going to do this by putting lettuce, bread, grass, cabbage and a pot-plant into the vivarium and leaving it overnight. In the morning we will see what the snails have eaten. This will tell us what snails like best. Glenn thinks that the snails will like the lettuce best, but everyone else thinks that cabbage will be the one.*

A specific focus does not preclude other observations, but does encourage children to hone in on specific information. This assists learning. Predicting expected outcomes gives loose guidelines for collecting information. (What I think will happen.)

By clarifying what they expect to happen, the children are examining their own ideas and expectations that they can then refer to and refine as further learning takes place. During the investigation some of their expectations will be confirmed, others will be challenged.

> *We were right the snails did like cabbage, but Glenn was right too because the snails ate lots of lettuce as well. They didn't eat much grass but ate some of the rhubarb leaves. The snail that escaped ate the corner of Mrs Feely's poster, so snails must like eating paper too.*

These children have confirmed some of their expectations and incorporated new ideas into the framework of their understandings about snails. By recording their initial predictions they were able to return at a later time and reflect on them.

WRITING DURING SCIENCE INVESTIGATIONS

I ask children to write and draw during an investigation because it helps them to observe more closely and to remember what has happened.

Writing is a useful tool to use during the investigation. Taking notes and filling in tables helps children to collect information that will be needed for interpreting and communicating after the investigation is over.

For example, during an investigation about the number and type of animals living in the school grounds, each child was asked to collect information for a survey which involved placing hoops in various parts of the yard and recording the animals they found as the basis for compiling a class chart.

Drawing is a powerful aid to use in focusing observation. Asking children to look at and draw a snail showing how it moves encourages close examination and promotes the idea of children making the discoveries themselves. Drawing accurately in this fashion is a sophisticated task in many ways, but children become very adept at it if they do it regularly while actually observing things.

Recording using a comic strip format is very useful for older children while involved in explorations.

Using this technique it is possible to get observations down fairly quickly as they occur. The artwork then provides a concise reference for other kinds of writing which may be attempted later. This technique for collecting information enables those children who are not confident writers to collect information — without losing sight of the task amid the difficulties of letter formation, spelling and grammar. In addition to these reasons, children seem to enjoy this way of collecting their observations.

The type of information to be collected usually indicates the style of writing that is most appropriate. For example, if children are testing the elasticity of a range of balls by measuring how high they bounce a table may be the most useful way to record findings.

Ball type	Dropped from 1 m	Dropped from 1.5 m	Dropped from 2 m
Tennis			
Basketball			
Table tennis			

Using such tables is a skill that children need to be taught. This can be done through teacher demonstration, filling in tables as a class and by children completing tables prepared by the teacher. Looking at how tables are constructed is essential. Identifying the components of such tables assists children to both read them and fill them in.

Getting children to formulate their own charts is more difficult. Careful discussion beforehand about what information is to be collected will help. For example, if investigating the acidity of different foodstuffs, children need to record the food tested against the colour the indicator turned and the acidity or basicity that this indicates. Encouraging children to devise and then use their charts leads to them identifying problems in their measurement tool and modifying it to make a more useful recording device. Providing photocopied grids can alleviate the time-consuming task of ruling up the table.

Developing focus questions as a framework for note-taking is also a useful means for encouraging recording during the investigation:

Which animals live in the tanbark?

How many legs do the animals have?

How many animals can fly?

These questions often grow naturally out of the pre-investigation talk mentioned previously.

Children should also be encouraged to set their own focus questions. If investigating the animal life in the schoolyard, a record sheet may be devised to assist in note-taking while observing first hand. For example:

Big animals that live in trees.
Small animals that live in trees.
Animals that live in the tanbark.
Animals that live in the classroom.
Animals that are in the garden.

It is important to choose the most appropriate means of enhancing learning and information collection during the investigation. Drawing may be useful when collecting information about the number of legs animals in the schoolyard have, but may not be all that useful when finding out how long a bubble lasts. Selection of measuring instruments is part of the science process. The forms of writing that children are asked to use during science investigations should be appropriate to the task and useful to the children. They will then be very happy to engage in these writing tasks.

WRITING TO COMMUNICATE IN SCIENCE

After the science investigation is completed, the information collected and conclusions drawn need to be recorded. This enables the children to communicate their new ideas and knowledge to others. It also enables them to clarify their thinking and to see for themselves what they have achieved.

The type of writing that scientists engage in is very specific. The nature of the task and the need for others to be able to replicate the experiment means that the writing must also be clear.

Children need to learn the best way to communicate for different audiences. When children share their results with an audience questions and discussion quickly arise. This is especially the case if each child has developed their own investigations and experiments.

'I don't understand what you did here Sarah.'

'We did the same experiment and that didn't happen for us.'

'Can we try that way of doing it? It's a better way than the way our group did it.'

Capitalising on these responses can lead children to become more critical of their own writing and to want to find better ways of communicating.

'What were you trying to communicate here Sarah? How could you have changed it to make it easier for your readers to understand?'

'Two of our investigation team have different results, how can we find out how this occurred?'

'What is it about this piece of work that communicates well enough for another group to want to use this experiment themselves?'

Of course developing effective writing in science, as with any other type of effective writing, takes time and practice. Teacher modelling, examination of other science writing and experimentation are all important elements in developing children's understanding of the writing process in science. Making children aware of the conventions of such writing can be done through providing a range of examples for children to use in identifying the elements involved. Retellings, in which the children read and then write the piece again while attempting to maintain accuracy and form, helps the children focus on the form and to develop the skills of this type of writing themselves.

Writing in science takes time to develop and refine. It does not happen overnight.

There are many forms of writing that children can engage in after science experiences.

Writing experiments for other children: 'The disappearing water experiment.'

Reports: 'Spiders in our schoolyard.'

Procedural texts: 'How to build an elastic-band powered boat.'

Explanations: 'How does your torch work?'

Flow charts.

This list is not exhaustive and is intended merely to provide a range of ideas about the type of writing children may be involved in following science investigations. Some children develop ideas about science. Others build on science ideas to develop skills in writing.

Conventional forms of scientific writing are, of course, not the only written response that children can make to their experiences in science. Other types of writing should be encouraged as well. Descriptive writing about things such as bubbles and weather can lead children to record their 'scientific' knowledge in a different form. A poem about a snail can only be enriched by the close observation of its movement and habitat.

EVALUATING THROUGH CHILDREN'S WRITING

The writing children engage in after science experiences is a rich source of information for evaluating the learning that has taken place. The language used by the children must be sensitively considered so that clues about the child's understanding of both science and writing are gleaned.

Children's writing after science experiences provides insights into each child's understanding of the science involved.

After finding a way to put paper under water without getting it wet, Karen writes:

When I put the cup in the water it worked because some air pressure pushed the water down so that the water did not reach the paper.

Karen has learned something about air pressure. She uses 'air pressure', then explains that it pushes. This tells me that she is developing an understanding of one of the properties of air.

After building and testing paper planes Marc wrote:

My plane did work because I built it a special way with tail enders to keep balance.

Marc has made some keen observations about the aerodynamics of his plane and the need to provide balance, but he lacks the words to express it clearly. Talking with Marc about his models while he is building them and reflecting back to him his ideas with some new words would be of great assistance.

Children's writing after science provides insights into their level of confidence and attitude:

'I don't know how it works because I don't know.'

'It didn't work because it was a dumb boat anyway.'

These children are expressing frustration and a lack of confidence. It could be with the exploration itself or with the writing task — the lack of words to express what they experienced. Providing some early assistance to get the investigation off to a good start may overcome these difficulties and will provide the teacher with more information.

Science is a rich source for learning in all curriculum areas. Writing enhances and is enhanced by science experiences. Children can gain satisfaction if the writing is relevant and useful to them. Teachers can also glean a great deal of knowledge about the knowledge and skills of their children by consideration of such writing.

Lesley Wing Jan

I would like the point to be considered that while children need to learn the ways language is used in science, to use language to learn about science and to be exposed to the implicit and explicit modelling of the ways of writing in science; they should also have the opportunity to select their own ways of recording information in this subject. The teacher's role is crucial to the development of these objectives.

NB: 'Implicit modelling' refers to the reading to, with and by children of various forms. 'Explicit modelling' involves the composing of a writing form for, with or by the children to show them how it is constructed.

SCENE

We had reached the end of a unit of work based on the topic Energy during which the children had investigated the sources, uses and nature of energy. During the unit the children had conducted experiments involving wind, water, solar and chemical energy. They had created open and closed circuits using batteries, globes and wire as well as other related activities. They had read a variety of information on energy ranging from pamphlets, tables of information, encyclopaedia entries, books, newspaper articles and interview summaries. Some of the written activities included recording procedures for and observations of experiments; completing Learning Log entries involving reflections on their understandings; creating concept maps; writing reports; labelling diagrams and taking notes. All these writing forms being as expected in science.

At the conclusion of the unit, some of the children wrote brochures extolling the features of energy-efficient homes, scripts for television advertisements for energy conservation and stories about future energy sources.

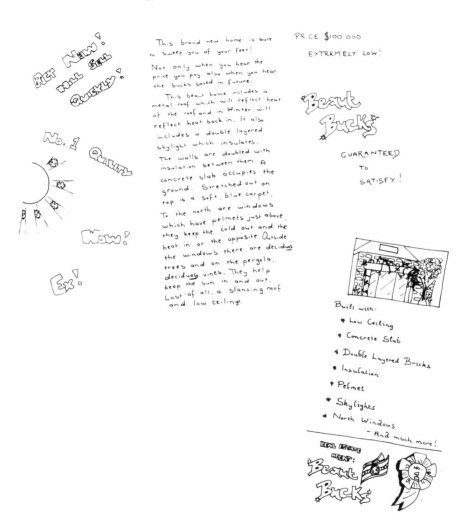

A BROCHURE WRITTEN DURING STUDY OF THE ENERGY UNIT.

Although these children had presented their knowledge in writing forms not usually associated with science, they had also explicitly demonstrated their understandings of the topic as effectively as those children who chose to write in the more traditional forms demonstrated during the unit of work.

WRITING TO MAKE MEANING ACROSS THE CURRICULUM

While we, as teachers, are comfortable with the writing process in our classroom writing workshops, we must ensure than the writing process is seen to be important and indeed valued across all curriculum areas. Writing across the curriculum must not be relegated to mere completion of worksheets or to the recipe-type formula as expected by some teachers of science.

As children participate in purposeful activities within each of the content/subject areas, they need to be able to discover, experiment with and understand the language unique to the topic.

Calkins (1986) claims that although children in the USA spend 44 per cent of their classroom time writing, only 3 per cent of their time is spent actually composing, which requires the child to be actively engaged in thinking, sorting and organising while writing. The remaining 41 per cent of their time writing is spent completing writing tasks that require minimum questioning, reflection or personal responses to their learning.

Opportunities need to be provided for children to use language to fulfil their purposes and needs within a subject area, and as they are using it enable them to discover, practise and refine the written language form that best meets their needs at the time.

WRITING IN AND ABOUT SCIENCE

If teachers recognise that children must write to learn, then they also need to recognise the power of writing to help children organise their beliefs, thoughts, impressions and understandings about science.

Our school programs need to be structured so that children not only learn about the language of science, but also use language to learn about science and to reflect on their learning of both science and language. The writing tasks that children are required to complete in science need to ensure than the children are using writing in authentic situations that will help them organise their learning, as well as help them learn about different writing forms for different purposes and audiences.

Science is a subject often viewed by many teachers as requiring a precise and objective language form. The language skills required in science are the same as any other inquiry-based learning activity. Language is used to identify, describe, list, classify, compare, observe and predict. These purposes of language are not unique to science, but some of the forms of language, such as scientific reports, research questions and procedural writing, are more common in this subject area than others. Some of the vocabulary associated with science is complex and demanding and should only be used in realistic contexts if the children are to extend their word knowledge and usage. Science is a process of making connections and communicating these connections, and the use of language for that purpose is very important, even if it is not scientifically written.

The modelling of the various language forms used in science helps children not only gain scientific knowledge, but also gain knowledge of how language works and how to use language to learn. Modelling can be implicit in which texts related to science are read to, with and by the children, or it may be explicit through the composing of a text for, with or by the children to show them how scientific data can be recorded.

NARRATIVE AND SCIENCE

Teachers need to help children gain meaning from their experiences, to organise their knowledge and make connections between learning in different subject areas. They also need to make connections between prior and newly gained knowledge. The understanding of concepts and facts are not only acquired objectively: they are formed through the learner's reaction to an experience. These reactions may often be recounted in the narrative form, which is a natural language form of young learners and adults alike. If narratives help children become actively engaged in the learning process, then this form must not be dismissed as irrelevant in science teaching and learning.

Wells (1986) recognises the narrative as being a powerful way of helping learners process new experiences or information:

> *Very young children, it is readily accepted, find it easier to assimilate new facts when they are presented within a framework of a story.*

When we were experimenting with magnets, I read *Magnet Magic* (Pigdon) to some Grade Three children in order to discover and explore the properties of magnets. Through the shared reading of this simple narrative the children were able to grasp very basic understandings about magnets and magnetism. Even though the information was not set out in any form typical of scientific writing, the important facts were able to be recorded in a meaningful way.

A shared reading of *The Magic School Bus Inside the Earth* (Cole, 1987) not only provided the children with an engrossing tale, but also provided plenty of factual material to enable them to develop their concepts and understandings of the subject. Prior to the reading of the book, the children were asked to record what they knew about the centre of the Earth. At the conclusion of the shared reading, they were then asked to record what they had learnt from the book. Their entries indicated a greater knowledge of the subject.

James

Before –
* It is liquid rock
* It is very hot
* Its proper name is the 'core'
* It is where volcanoes come from

After –
* The core is made of liquid metal
* The earth is divided into three parts underground.
* The centre part is made of hot metal and melted
* The crust is made of cool rock and soil.
* There are more kinds of rock in the crust
* The two centre parts of the earth are called the inner 'and the 'outer core'

THE CHILDREN'S BEFORE AND AFTER CONCEPTS.

It can be daunting for a child to grapple with the structure and use of a prescribed form of language while still trying to make sense of an experience. It is essential that children are able to explore feelings and attitudes within the content areas and this is often done best in the narrative form. Narratives are a part of children's language since their first attempts at communication. Narratives involve a sequence of activities or events that are linked and involve:

- an orientation to the setting, participants, activity or time;

- a complication or problem that needs to be described;

- a resolution or conclusion for the activity described.

Many experiences can be described in narrative form. Life is a narrative that is told in many different ways according to the narrator and the audience.

Science is also an ever-changing narrative as more facts and information emerge as a result of inquiry. Science as a narrative enables the children to explain and interpret their experiences and clarify their own ideas within an authentic and familiar language form.

Reading science as a narrative not only models this form of writing but also helps develop further the children's scientific knowledge.

Composing either a narrative or language form more common to science (as a result of an inquiry approach to a science activity) involves similar problem-solving activities. In both the narrative and the more formalised language form the child must:

- identify the knowledge that he/she has gained and wishes to communicate;

- select and organise the relevant information;

- write an introduction in order to orientate the audience;

- create an accurate account of the activity;

- create a conclusion that makes both forms complete.

For example:

Sally, who was in Grade Six, showed an extreme interest in ants and avidly read as much as possible about them. She also observed the behaviour of ants, read about the setting up of an ant farm and generally became informed about the subject. Sally chose to write a narrative called 'Jam on the Window Sill'. This piece of writing incorporated her knowledge of the subject into a well-written narrative that demonstrated not only her excellent command of this writing form, but also her logical and systematic organisation of knowledge about these social insects.

Tan could sense the ant in front of her. Now she would get home quickly. It was hard for her to find her way home on her own because like most ants, she had poor vision. As she arrived at her nest, the Soldier ants watched her go by.

A SAMPLE OF SALLY'S WRITING.

The use of narrative allows for personalised responses to learning. It also requires children to organise information and formulate beliefs and understandings and to use this assimilated knowledge to communicate these.

WRITING FOR MANY PURPOSES IN SCIENCE

I believe that while children need to be exposed to the unique forms of language associated with science, teachers also need to observe children as learners and allow them scope to use the language that best personalises their responses to learning.

Sometimes children may use narrative to organise their learning in science, or they may use other forms not usually associated with the subject in order to organise, refine or present their knowledge of science.

Using the language of science may aid vocabulary development and help children use language more accurately, but we must also not minimise the importance of creative, imaginative and subjective responses to experiences in science.

Expressive and descriptive language must not be sacrificed for more precise scientific language. Descriptive narratives can reveal the importance of particular experiences to an individual learner. For example, as part of a unit of work on 'Water' our class set up an experiment to demonstrate the effect of evaporation on salt water. Karen, along with the rest of the class, observed the process over a period of days. When it came to recording her observations, Karen enthusiastically described in detail the colour, texture, taste and shape of the salt crystals that had formed on the saucer and then wrote about her previous experience in Grade Four of growing sugar crystals. She had made some personal links between the two activities. The remainder of the class recounted (described the sequence of events associated with the process) and while recording the presence of crystals, did not respond to the experience in the same way as Karen did. Some children were also asked to rewrite the above experiment in procedural form, using the accepted scientific format of aim, apparatus, procedure, observations and conclusion. The purpose for writing in this prescribed form was to ensure that the experiment could be accurately replicated. Thus it became important to model the acceptable format for experiments as well as introducing the correct terms for each part. The purpose and audience for this writing form was different to that of writing a recount of the experiment for personal record or for a known audience.

The transfer of acquired knowledge is an indication of the children's understanding of the subject area. Sometimes scientific language used in one setting will be used in a new and apparently unrelated task. This was clearly demonstrated to me when two Grade Three boys began a jointly constructed text about ghosts. 'Not another fantasy,' was my initial reaction. But their pre-writing planning revealed that they were going to write an explanation about ghosts. Even though they chose a fictional topic, they wrote in the structure of explanations and included vocabulary that had been introduced during a science topic, such as species and classification.

Modelling can be a powerful way of helping children process their knowledge. I read to my Grade Six class, a series of narratives that contained a great deal of factual knowledge within a fictional framework. We refer to these texts as Narrative Information. As part of a research task about the environment, a small group had been reading about conservation and the need to recycle. Louie, a member of the group, had been required to present an oral

7 HOW A GHOST IS BORN AND WHAT TYPE OF SPECIES A GHOST BELONGS TO

A ghost belongs to the species whiteses.

Now this is how a ghost is born. The mother ghost puts a bit of her slime on the ground and the slime just shoots up into the air like a rocket taking off but not quite as fast.

When this is completed you have a new ghost.

A SAMPLE OF WRITING ABOUT GHOSTS.

report on the recyling process for aluminium cans and the impact on the environment. She duly completed this task and to my delight chose to write about the process during writers' workshop (where the children have complete ownership over the choice of topic, form and purpose of their writing). Louie wrote her information in the form of a narrative in which she assumed the role of an aluminium can and described the process of recycling. So she had used the inquiry process to gain the information and had then chosen to record it in narrative form.

Given the opportunity children can differentiate and employ many different language forms for different purposes and audiences, provided they have been exposed to these forms.

In our science time we were working on a unit about animal behaviours. The children had gained much of the information they required from the charts, tables and diagrams used in many books related to the topic. In writers' workshop Rohani, a very keen writer, had been writing a narrative involving a penguin as the main character. She had drawn on her experiences as a spectator of the nightly penguin parade at Phillip Island. At the end of the narrative, Rohani changed her use of language to summarise the characteristics of penguins in table form. When asked why she had done this she said the narrative was written for younger children and the table of information was for older people to find out

G'day I'm Ann Mac your everyday Coke can.
Aluminium Coke can of course. Here I am
sitting on the supermarket shelf for the 23rd
time, I think. Oh well who's counting. Getting
back to the point I'm here to tell you all about
how I've been recycled and how it happened to
me.

A SAMPLE OF LOUIE'S WRITING.

important information about penguins. Thus Rohani had recognised the purpose of the two forms of writing she had freely chosen to use, even though both forms revealed her knowledge on the subject.

The fantasy element of science must not be overlooked if we wish to encourage children to explore the possible effects of science or technology and predict the implications of scientific advances. Science fiction is based on fact and the possibilities are only limited by the writer's imagination. This imagination would not be exercised if the more traditional forms of writing in science were the only forms available to the writer.

PLANNING FOR WRITING AND LEARNING IN SCIENCE

To ensure that writing within a subject area helps learners gain knowledge as well as promote and control active thinking, there needs to be a purpose and appropriate context for each writing task. The following is an outline of how I plan to include writing in science.

Once a topic has been selected I list the understandings, concepts, and skills I wish the children to gain from the unit. The topic may arise from an expressed interest from the children or it may arise from a need I see in the overall program. An initial experience, such as an excursion, film, discussion or experiment, is conducted and from this the focus questions for the investigation are formed with and by the children.

Resources are then collected and activities planned that will help answer the focus questions and build up the children's understandings of the topic.

The specific language focuses, such as vocabulary, text forms and spelling, that can be drawn from the topic are listed, and I plan how writing could best be used to help children develop their knowledge of science and of language.

During the unit I model the appropriate language forms for the activities, such as note-taking, reading and writing factual texts. These are conducted within the context of the activity being conducted and/or the concept being explored.

I also model how I need to write to make an experience meaningful to me. This reflective writing is a good way of organising information and making connections between new and prior knowledge.

Through modelling, the children's repertoire is extended and they are able to choose the appropriate writing form for their personal purpose. Specific writing tasks are set if I require the matching of a writing form to a specific activity.

I evaluate the children's progress through observation of them as they work both as scientists and as writers. Anecdotal records help me keep track of their development. Examination of the children's written work often tells me if and how they use scientific terms and knowledge, if they can explain the processes, if they really understand the topic and if they reflect on their learning.

MATCHING TEXTS TO PURPOSES

The planning procedure outlined combines a workable blend of writing in the form unique to the subject area and the provision of choice of writing form, purpose and audience. This approach facilitates the development of the children's knowledge about science and the language of science, as well as ensuring that they use written language to learn about the subject. The following outline of a unit demonstrates how writing in science does not have to be to a prescribed formula.

A unit of work that was conducted with my Grade Six class was based on the heart. The focus questions were concerned with the structure, function and care of the heart. The unit was planned so that each objective was supported with a science investigation and associated language activities. For example, one objective was for the children to investigate the differences in pulse rates at rest and during activity. The children were to measure and graph pulse rates of the whole class during both rest and activity. The language activities associated with the investigation involved explaining the graph, reporting on what was found, labelling a diagram to indicate the pulse points and describing how the information was collected. During each of these activities the children were using the vocabulary associated with the subject, as well as approximating the various language forms.

At the end of the unit of work the children were asked to present their understandings in a written format. Throughout the year the children had been exposed, both implicitly and explicitly, to many different forms of writing, ranging from charts, narratives and procedural texts to reports. So it was no surprise that the children were able to record their knowledge in such a range of writing forms. There were recounts of the activities associated with the unit, cinquain poems, charts about heart health, persuasive writing about the need for exercise, explanations on the function of the heart, factual reports, procedural texts and

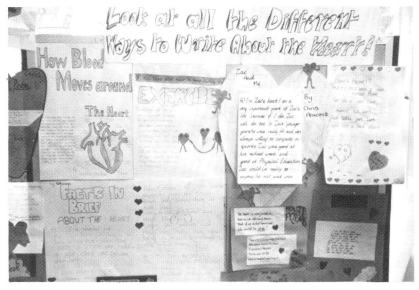

DISPLAY OF WRITING FORMS USED.

engaging narratives that included many of the facts discussed. Each child, through the use of language, had processed the information gained during the unit and had personalised their response to the experience.

IMPLICATIONS FOR TEACHING

I believe that teachers need to take an active role in ensuring that children are aware of the different forms of writing for different purposes. At times the children may need to approximate and refine these different language forms according to their stage of language development and the degree of complexity of the task involved across the curriculum. This implies that teachers need to be aware of the unique uses of language within specific subject areas and model these as appropriate and intervene in the child's learning cycle as required. Having said this, I believe there must be scope for children to interpret and unravel their understandings in their own choice of form. The narrative, both factual and fictional, must not be overlooked as an appropriate writing form to help children organise and reflect on their learning.

Just as I have chosen the form I wish to use to define, organise and convey my thoughts to you about the use of the many forms of writing in science; so should children be given the opportunity to make similar choices.

References

Calkins, L. (1986), *The Art of Teaching Writing*, Heinemann, Portsmouth, NH.
Wells, Gordon (1986), *The Meaning Makers: Children Learning Language and Using Language to Learn*, Heinemann, Portsmouth, NH.

Bibliography

Anstey, Michele (1988), 'Integrating Writing and Inquiry', *PEN*, **66**, PETA, NSW.
Ministry of Education (1987), *The Science Framework: P–10*, Curriculum Branch, Victoria.
Turner, Judy et al., 'Language Learning While Learning Science', *PEN*, **8**, PETA, NSW.
Wing, Jan L. (1991), *Write Ways: Modelling Writing Forms*, OUP, Melbourne.
Zubrick, A., 'Oral Narrative in Young Children: Implications for Early Reading and Writing', *Australian Journal of Reading*, **2**, 97–105.

Children's Books Referred To in Text

Cole, Joanne (1987), *The Magic School Bus Inside the Earth*, Ashton Scholastic, New York.
Pigdon, N., *Magnet Magic*, Southern Cross, Macmillan, Melbourne.

Philip, aged seven, poured over books about birds which he had borrowed from the school and local libraries. Birds were his latest obsession. He wrote his own book about birds of prey and concluded it with, 'I love birds of prey'. Books are an important source of pleasure and information to Philip and they play an active part in any science program. The emphasis here being on 'part'. With the volume of science books available to schools increasing at an amazing rate, teachers are faced with not only selection choices, but a re-examination of how books can best serve children in their pursuit of making sense of the world.

Children need to see themselves as responsible directors of their own learning, not just as receptacles of the information contained in science texts. This implies moving beyond the science text.

In Chapter 5, Nea Stewart Dore draws distinctions between a knowledge-making and a knowledge-duplicating reading of the scientific world. She goes on to outline different kinds of science texts and their purposes.

Many science textbooks show science as being a body of knowledge. Something that 'is' with the human elements of the scientist thinking and doing left out. Beverly Derewianka examines one secondary science textbook to highlight the problems of science texts: the high rate of new vocabulary introduced, the text structure, the dense information load and the effect of nominalisation.

Jo Coffey uses a wide range of books as part of her science program at Middle Park Primary School. She tells us about some of her favourites, why she likes them and how they are used during incidental and planned science activities.

Nea Stewart-Dore

WHAT SCIENTISTS SAY

We use language to investigate and report science.

For physicists Bohm and Peat (1987), language is integral to

> *...the very act of scientific perception. Scientists...constantly engage in a form of internal dialogue with the whole structure of their particular discipline. In this dialogue a scientist raises questions and meets points of view which are attributed to other scientists...In addition...scientists are actively engaged in their daily work with a social exchange of ideas and opinions through discussions, lectures, conferences and published papers.*

Likewise, Wahlqvist (1989), a medical scientist, observes that

> *...in science, it is increasingly impossible to do work alone...[Besides] needing a team around one to do work, it is very important...that debate, discussion, review of primary data can be taking place all the time.*

Yet the uses of language in science are problematic, as well. Critical of how scientific writing conventions are confining, impersonal and indifferent 'to anything like the display of a unique human author in scientific exposition', the theoretical physicist, Mermin (1990) for example, claims that as a result:

The reading of most scientific papers [has been transformed] into an act of tedious drudgery, [and has] also deprived scientists of some powerful tools for enhancing their clarity in communicating matters of great complexity.

The Canadian geneticist Suzuki (1990), concurs.

By emphasizing a proper way to do an experiment and to write it up, we create a myth about how [scientific] research is done. And we lose all the passion that makes the scientific enterprise so worthwhile.

He proposes (1990), that we 'think [not] in terms of [science but of] *exploration, discovery, connections*' to 'find ways to instil excitement and interest' in the world of science, especially in schools.

In these excerpts, eminent scientists talk of the ways in which language is used to negotiate scientific inquiry, and of some of the limitations in 'writing up' and communicating its outcomes conventionally. To relate these ideas to young children's investigations of the natural world and to secondary students' experiences of school science, I find it useful to distinguish (with help from Friere and Macedo (1987)) two kinds of reading. They are *reading the scientific world* and *reading the science word*.

Two vignettes illustrate these ways of reading science. Each occurs in a different social context. As a result, different kinds of texts are used for different purposes. Following a brief examination of the nature and uses of texts read in two contexts, some ideas for extending students' experience of a variety of 'science world' texts are proposed.

READING THE SCIENTIFIC WORLD

'Guess what we found in Gran's pool over the holidays?'

I pondered 7-year-old David's question, seeking clues to its possible answer. I knew that his grandmother's backyard pool nudges bushland where David discovers wildlife specimens periodically, and that he had been out with a toad-busters group to help eradicate cane toads. I put two and two together.

'Was it an army of drowned cane toads?'

David grimaced, but conceded grudgingly, 'You're warm.'

'How about a green tree frog, then?'

'No-o-o! Eggs! A big mass of frogs' eggs! And do you know what kind they were?'

'I only know about toads and green tree frogs,' I admitted reluctantly.

David feigned exasperation. 'Nuh. They were Ornate Burrowing frogs' eggs,' he proclaimed. 'And do you know how we found that out? The man from the Frog Society told us.'

Intrigued, I asked, 'How can you tell what kind of frogs they are from the eggs?'

David giggled. 'You can't! We found a frog in the pool too! And we took it home and the eggs in some dam water and guess what? Um, next day they were tadpoles! And they grew and then their tails shortened and they grew legs and we watched them grow into frogs and that took about um, two, no, um, nearly three weeks. They're really beautiful colours, orange and brown. The orange bits are like triangles, and guess where they like to live? In bark and leaf litter. They burrow in the leaves. And do you know how you can tell the difference between frogs' eggs and cane toads' eggs? Well, it's easy. If you see a white mass, sort of like a clear white mass of eggs bunched up all together, that means they're frogs' eggs because cane toads lay their eggs in long strings and they've got black dots in the middle of each one.'

Name: Ornate Buroing

~~Couler (Collser)~~
Colūr: brown with orange triagles.

Habitat: bark and leave litter.

Stages of groth: eggs to tadpole to tadpole with back legs to tadpole with front and back tale will soften if theres no rock they will drown.

Egg masses: frog eggs are layed in a mass toad egg are layed in a ~~strind~~ strines.

Edentafing ~~frog~~ tadpoles: frog tadpole are clear and toad tadpoles are black.

Male and Female: the female is biger liter coloured the male is darker and smaller.

Mateing call: the Mateing call is a deep brping sownd.

David : 7 years
23 February 1991

DAVID'S DESCRIPTION.

'That's wonderful! I'm sure Uncle Colin would like to hear about them. Maybe you could write to him?'

David paused, then suggested reluctantly, 'Uh, I could write a little description.'

Later he drafted the text, pausing only to complain, 'I forget what word says where frogs live.' I provided 'habitat' for him.

David's interest in frogs was spawned by helping Sean, a neighbour, collect insects to feed the frogs he bred in his frog house. That led to a family museum excursion to learn how to identify frog species and care for them in captivity. Given a dozen tadpoles to take home, the family was in the process of rearing them when David found the frog and its eggs in the swimming pool.

Interpretation

In this vignette, we glimpse David transacting information. He poses successive, predominantly rhetorical 'Guess what?' questions and 'Did you know that...' prefacing statements to review his zoological inquiry. He then synthesises factual data from different sources into a communicative report.

What texts constituted David's field activities and what were his purposes in using them? After mentally framing the question, 'What kind of frog is it?', David searched library books for pictorial and written evidence to identify and name his specimen. Unable to resolve the problem by that means, he observed, distinguished, described and discussed with others the frog's attributes; comparing and contrasting them with those of other frogs in his collection and with the textual information he had collected. With assistance, he consulted experts, including a member of the Brisbane Frog Society. The Society had advertised an information evening in the newspaper. That consultation, during which he listened to frog calls over the telephone, eliminated some possibilities. The collaborative conclusion drawn was that David's frog exhibited the features of the relatively rare species, *Limnodynastes ornatus*, or Ornate Burrowing frog.

David verified his identification by researching topic books which also yielded some 'frog stories' and poems that he enjoyed reading. Meanwhile, he observed his growing tadpoles' habits under varied conditions. The evolution of their colour, distribution and number of markings, as well as the comparative growth of different specimens were all observed. He hypothesised that colour and size differences distinguished males from females. Taking advice gleaned from his reading, David finally gave away most of his fully-grown frogs to people who could provide habitats where live food was available. As people took delivery, David advised and issued duplicated museum notes on the care of frogs and tadpoles.

David's field investigation occurred over a period of weeks. During that time, he practised scientific literacy: exploring, questioning, discovering and making connections to generate new knowledge. In identifying a particular frog's attributes, David emulated what zoologists do — perceiving, conceiving, sharing, shaping, expressing and communicating scientific meanings. He did this collaboratively in a responsive discourse community, challenging the frontiers of his, and others' knowledge-generating capacities.

Although we do not have access to what David may have written to assist his investigation, we know that he read (interpreted) both the natural and textual worlds of frogs extensively, using a variety of references, and generated, shaped and communicated his knowledge in many critically enquiring discussions.

READING THE SCIENCE WORD

Sharon began the Science lesson. 'Right everyone. Turn to page 70. Remember, we're looking at amphibians. Last time we learned that amphibians are animals that...Michael, what do you remember about amphibians?'

'Uh...(pause)...they're cold-blooded?'

'O.K. They're cold-blooded. Who can add to what Michael's told us? What do you remember, Kate?'

'I wasn't here, Miss.'

'Oh, all right. Listen carefully then, so you can catch up. Robyn, can you help, er, add to the information we have about amphibians?'

'Well, I um, I got a bit confused.' ('Do they live um, on land and in the water?')

('Yeh, it doesn't make sense.')

('Why can't we cut up a toad?')

'Right. There's some confusion. We'll do a little bit of revision, then. Look back to page 70 and the notes, um the diagram we did or rather, added to on the board. You've got it in your books, like on the chart at the back. See how it says, there at the top of the page, the heading "Amphibians". Read it out, please John.'

John reads the heading, 'Amphibians'.

'Oh, keep going. Read the whole paragraph. Everyone watching.' John reads the following passage:

Amphibians

Amphibians are animals that can live in water or on land. They are poikilothermic or 'cold blooded'. Adult frogs have lungs like reptiles, birds and mammals. When in water, however, they can absorb oxygen through their slippery skins. They mostly eat animal food, usually insects and the like. Australia has about 120 species of frogs and one toad. This latter is the introduced cane toad of Queensland that has caused so much trouble. The skin of the cane toad is poisonous. If a cat or dog tries to eat a cane toad it can die. In other parts of the world there is another group of amphibians called salamanders and newts (Figure 4.29). All told, there are about 2,500 species of amphibians on Earth.

[Ash, et al. (1987), *Elements of Science: Book 1*, Longman Cheshire, Melbourne.]

'O.K. So what's the main idea here? What did we say was the point of talking about amphibians like this? It's very important, you know, so pay attention. It shows us how scientists go about, doing what, Angela? Are you listening? That's what we've been making our notes about. How scientists...'

Luc broke the interrogation chain. 'Miss, Miss! They class things, um in groups, different kinds of groups like here, frogs, they're animals with backbones like us.'

'Right, no need to call out. They classify whatever it is they are studying. That's really what we're looking at. How scientists classify, so if you look at our diagram, we added to it yesterday, turn to it everyone, if you look at that you'll see that frogs and toads fit into the amphibian class.'

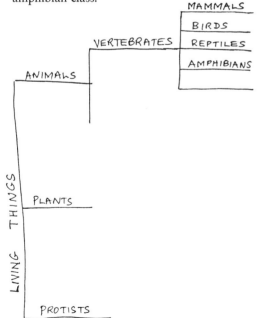

CLASSIFICATION TABLE.

Forty minutes later, fish too, had been described, classified and added to the chart, after Sharon had taken over the textbook reading.

Interpretation

Little is startling about this textbook-based science lesson. Its routines are replicated in many schools where numerous constraints restrict what will be taught, and how, and in what time frames. So what texts constitute Sharon's lesson and how are they used to learn about a class of amphibians?

The texts used in the lesson include students' memory scripts of the previous lesson's subject matter; a textbook passage; a published classification table and its chalkboard and student notebook duplication; and exchanges circumscribing literal question-answer 'text talk' (Cairney, 1989; 1990). Throughout the lesson, Sharon chooses what will be read, when, by whom and for what purpose, gently chastising those who disturb her routine.

To focus verbal transactions, Sharon poses 'What do you remember?', 'What can you add?' and 'How do scientists work?' questions to reaffirm conceptual links between bits of pooled information and items on a scientific classification table. The result is that students' encounters with the curriculum texts are fleeting and perfunctory, limited to recollection and literal re-readings to identify (from scant data) frogs' and toads' zoological classification.

Arguably, students must be familiar with the hierarchical structure and relational network of items on classification tables, since they are fundamental to the way natural scientists frame and express their understanding of the world. Recognising that, Sharon emphasises classification as being 'the point of talking about amphibians'. Yet her method of reconstructing the table is a-natural. Being decontextualised and being textbook-based, it is well removed from the field investigations that motivate and rationalise the naming and ordering of living things. This lesson, dominated by the exchange of factual information, has none of the excitement of David's quest for data to solve a self-generated classificatory problem.

KINDS OF TEXTS IN SCIENCE

Three categories of text are used for reading the scientific world and reading the science word. They are (1) Field Inquiry Texts; (2) School Science Textbooks; and (3) Knowledge Transmission Texts.

Field Inquiry Texts

When we investigate science, either in the field or in the laboratory, we read the scientific world. In the process of thinking about and carrying out our research, we form and express knowledge in spoken and written language. The texts that evolve purposefully at different stages during that process can be called Field Inquiry Texts. They are a component part of conducting an investigation.

Field Inquiry Texts include observation notes and speculative records as well as the 'written-up' forms of them. They express hypotheses, conditions, procedures, results, analytic and comparative discussions, and conclusions. 'Written-up' notes form the basis of edited reports published in professional journals which announce findings to colleagues. They inspire response, critical reviews and correspondence, such as rebuttals and replies in journals, and seminar and conference discussion papers. All of these writings are included in the category: Field Inquiry Texts.

It is from a synthesis of debated writings of reported research procedures and outcomes that ultimately, a 'body of knowledge' is sanctioned by the scientific community. That 'body of knowledge' comprises the theories, principles, laws, explanations and descriptions which express understanding of the nature of things. It is then collected into books of original texts (hence the word 'textbooks') written by pioneering scientists such as Galileo, Newton and Darwin. Thest 'textbooks' contain the information that becomes the point of departure for further research in the relevant branch of science. By consulting such reference material, scientists proceed in their research from where others left off (Kuhn, 1970), and students can access authoritative information.

School Science Textbooks

School Science Textbooks such as the one Sharon used, are descendants of collected original works. Used for instructing learners about the major *findings* of scientific investigation, the information in them is distilled, simplified and stripped of the signs of their contextualised, authoritative origins. As a result, School Science Textbooks necessarily comprise generalis-ations. They abstract from very complex operations, procedural steps for replicating simple laboratory experiments, as well as feature instructional aids such as chapter summaries, comprehension checks, and exercises or applied problem-solving activities.

Knowledge Transmission Texts

Another text type in the science field is the focused topic or theme book. I call them Knowledge Transmission Texts. When we read Knowledge Transmission Texts in science, we read the science word. That is, we read information *about* science matters written by others. We can read Knowledge Transmission Texts, as David did, to discover information and verify observations. In that sense, they can be used to confirm developing understandings of knowledge we are in the process of generating for ourselves.

Mostly, however, Knowledge Transmission Texts are used as sources for *gathering* information, rather than generating 'breakthrough' knowledge in the field. As do School Science Textbooks, Knowledge Transmission Texts summarise selected aspects of a field in discrete, topical chapters. Their inclusion in collections of literature-based curriculum resources for primary schools is increasingly apparent. Some titles in these collections comprise 'information reports' on natural and physical phenomena. Others include procedural directions for carrying out observations and experiments in instructional textbook fashion, thus offering a range of different kinds of Knowledge Transmission Texts.

There are, however, many other kinds of Knowledge Transmission Texts including:

1. Newspaper reports and feature articles announcing discoveries, exploring issues and dilemmas, profiling the work of a celebrated or controversial scientist, or charting the progress of explorations such as that of the Hubble telescope.

2. Popular and specialist magazine articles discussing scientific work and its ramifications for science and society.

3. Books, comprising autobiographies and biographies; illustrated descriptions or explanations of specific phenomena; field observation guides; print versions of radio talks and television series; and scientists' perspectives on the nature, function and consequences of scientific investigation.

4. Encyclopaedias, digests, 'libraries' or 'series', and specialist dictionaries.

Being willing and able to read the science word published in a wide range of texts is important to becoming scientifically literate. Unfortunately, many secondary students' classroom experiences with the science word is limited to those encountered in a teacher-selected and mediated textbook.

IMPLICATIONS FOR DEVELOPING SCIENTIFIC LITERACY

In secondary school text-based science programs, students' literate thinking in science must go beyond participating occasionally in interrogations of distilled science facts that are detailed in textbooks. Students must also apprehend the many other ways science ideas, processes, outcomes and effects can be shaped, expressed and communicated. That will involve them in a range of shared, guided and independent reading activities, which preferably will have been negotiated with them. For instance, students and teachers might collaborate to plan scientific literacy activities such as these:

1. Survey, list and talk about the range, types and purposes of scientific research writings in journals and compare and contrast these, as Mallow (1991) suggests, with 'popular'

writing about science topics in newspapers and specialist magazines.

2. Collect, display, read and discuss different kinds of texts and their uses in the science field. News reports, feature articles, science columns, newspaper special supplements, advertisements and cartoon strips can feature on bulletin boards. Magazines, journals, and books can be relocated in laboratory libraries for easy access.

3. Negotiate cross-curricula work requirements in language study, experimental science and analytic report writing using advertisements that assert scientific claims for the supremacy over others, of some household cleaning agents, cosmetics and toiletries, food nutrients, additives or preservatives. Or compare and contrast the way science topics and issues are treated in different media. Thus, students might analyse the structure and content of television documentaries, science series or investigative reports; the purposes and processes of inventors' competitions, or the representation of science issues in cartoons such as *Swamp* (ecological systems) or publicity campaigns such as *Greening Australia* (conservation).

4. Invite practising scientists to talk about and demonstrate the role of reading and writing in their daily work, or visit laboratories where scientists work amid data recorded in various forms, including electronic.

In planning text-based science programs, we should note the different functions of reading (and hence writing) in the field. A balanced science program would familiarise students with ways of reading both the scientific world and the science word, hence they would become increasingly aware of both the processes and products of scientific literacy. In this way, adolescents' experiences of science in school are likely to approximate more closely, how both scientists and young children use a range of written texts to construct knowledge for themselves.

References

Ash, J.M., Jess, T.J., Wilson, B.G., Heffernan, D.A. and Learmonth, M.S. (1987), *Elements of Science: Book 1*, Longman Cheshire, Melbourne.

Bohm, D. and Peat, F.D. (1987), *Science, Order and Creativity: A Dramatic New Look at the Creative Roots of Science and Life*, Bantam Books, New York.

Cairney, T.H. (1989), 'Text Talk: Helping students learn about language', *English in Australia*, 90, December.

Cairney, T.H. (1990), *Teaching Reading Comprehension: Meaning Makers at Work*, Open University Press, Milton Keynes.

Friere, P. and Macedo, D. (1987), *Literacy: Reading the word and the world*, Greenwood, Westport, CT.

Kuhn, T.S. (1970), *The Structure of Scientific Revolutions* (2nd edn.), University of Chicago Press, Chicago, IL.

Mallow, J.V. (1991), 'Reading Science', *Journal of Reading*, **34**, 5, 324–338.

Mermin, N.D. (1990), *Boojums All the Way Through: Communicating Science in a Prosaic Age*, Cambridge University Press, New York.

Suzuki, D. (1990), *Inventing the Future: Reflections on Science. Technology and Nature*, Allen & Unwin, Sydney.

Wahlqvist, M. (1989), 'Scandals and Winds of Change' in Williams, R. (ed.), *The Uncertainty Principle: Australian Scientists Talk about their World and our Future*, Australian Broadcasting Corporation, Sydney.

Beverly Derewianka

As with the reading of any text, the reading of a science textbook involves a complex of behaviours and strategies. The degree of success will depend upon factors such as prior knowledge of the subject matter and how this is developed in the classroom, the educational and cultural background of the student, motivational issues, and various other factors. This chapter will, however, concentrate on the text itself and how it might be implicated in the reading process.

For many years now, we have been aware of the important role that oral language plays in learning. We know how valuable it is for students to come to an understanding of a concept or topic through 'talking it out'. In science, in particular, the oral mode is ideal for the sort of exploration that is characteristic of scientific inquiry. Because of its face-to-face, dynamic nature, oral language allows us to ask questions, to make suggestions, to follow up on leads, to change our minds mid-sentence if necessary, to challenge others, to form opinions, to offer tentative explanations and to get immediate feedback. This is the sort of give-and-take that goes on in small groups as students wrestle with problems, in the lab as they carry out experiments and on field trips as they observe and comment. It is this spoken inter-action that allows for meanings to be jointly constructed as the participants bounce their embryonic understandings off one another.

While we might argue that opportunities for observation, hands-on activities, problem-solving, group work and other explorations that use oral language are invaluable in coming to grips with the nature and subject matter of science, we also need to acknowledge the constraints of secondary schools and to concede that timetables won't always permit this sort of open-ended, serendipitous inquiry. As more demands are placed on students' time and as they begin to deal with more abstract concepts, students increasingly need to be able to carry out such inquiry through the written medium. They need to be able to access understandings 'vicariously', from text rather than always from first-hand, practical experience.

Reading enables a different sort of inquiry. Unlike oral language, it is independent of any immediate context. We do not have to rely solely on those with whom we are able to interact in a face-to-face situation. Reading, therefore, gives us access to the thinking of scientists who may be distant in time or in location. We can commune with significant historical figures such as Galileo, Darwin and Einstein, or keep in touch with contemporary issues and innovations through the writings of Suzuki, Kuhn or Asimov. And because we are not constrained by the immediacy of speech, we have greater flexibility in terms of when and where we access this knowledge.

THE NATURE AND ROLE OF TEXTBOOKS

When children read factual texts in primary school, they have often selected a book that suits their particular interests, or they have borrowed a number of books in order to find information for a particular project. These children are dipping in and out of a wide variety of books and different types of texts throughout the year. In secondary school, it is the textbook that becomes a major source of information. In many ways this is restricting. Textbooks tend to present scientific knowledge in a reductionist way as 'given', unchanging, and readily apprehended. They also give the impression that the scientific enterprise can be neatly prescribed, categorised and replicated.

Having said that, however, textbooks in the secondary school are a reality with which we need to come to terms. I would like to suggest in this chapter that there is a role for science textbooks — alongside the multitude of other texts, oral and written, that participate in the scientific discourse of the classroom. The textbook provides a constant point of reference. They are designed to systematically develop understandings over a period of time.

Most are written as series, allowing for a cyclical build up of knowledge over a number of years. Basic concepts are introduced, then elaborated upon and extended in later volumes. A textbook provides readily available support as the teacher attempts to develop complex concepts. A textbook can be taken home and mulled over at leisure, clarifying issues raised in the classroom, filling in gaps, and treating topics in greater depth than is possible in the give-and-take of classroom interaction. The textbook is a resource that enables students to consolidate and extend their knowledge as independent learners.

In many schools the science textbook has been put aside — not in favour of the wide-ranging, 'authentic' texts mentioned above, but to be replaced by even more reductionist 'ditto sheets' or teacher-dictated notes. In some cases this is due to the cost of textbooks. Schools can often only afford to buy a class set for the whole grade, to be distributed as needed during lessons. Because of this, students never develop a sense of 'ownership' of the book: a familiarity with its contents, the habit of delving into it to satisfy curiosity or to follow up a point of interest or puzzlement. Their attention instead is directed to a certain paragraph on a certain page, which might be read aloud or copied into their exercise books.

In other cases, textbooks have fallen from favour because teachers believe that they are too hard for the students to read. This belief is often based on the commonly held assumption among secondary teachers that students entering secondary school know how to read. In one sense this is true, but while they may have developed the 'basic skills' and be able to cope adequately with the sorts of reading typically found in primary school, the reading demands of secondary school are sometimes dramatically different. Children who were successful readers in primary school often find themselves in trouble when faced with secondary texts. The narratives and beautifully illustrated, entertaining factual books aimed at primary school children generally give way to densely written, relatively technical textbooks. In order to comprehend these texts, students need to be initiated, not only into the new fields of knowledge, but also into how textbooks work.

Rather than discard the textbook because it is perceived to be too hard, how might we instead support students in their reading of textbooks?

READING THE TEXTBOOK

Let us take a sample excerpt from a widely used junior secondary science textbook in order to illustrate what is involved in reading a science textbook.

> During the last part of the nineteenth century, and during the early 1900s scientists were able to find out what atoms are made of. They found that atoms are made of even smaller particles called electrons, protons and neutrons. In the centre of the atom is the nucleus containing the uncharged neutrons and the positively charged neutrons [sic]. One widely used picture of atoms shows the negatively charged electrons moving around the nucleus in circular paths (Figure 3D). We now know that the atom is really much more complex than this.
>
> ### Elements
> Elements are made of atoms. Each of the 106 or so elements is made from one type of atom. Each one of these types of atoms is different from the atoms of the other

elements. One such difference is that each of the types of atoms has a different number of electrons. Thus an atom of carbon (C) has six electrons, and so has a different size and different chemical properties from those of an atom of oxygen (O) with eight electrons.

Compounds

Compounds are made from molecules. Each type of compound has its own molecule. Each type of molecule is made of a set number of atoms joined together. Thus, a molecule of water (H_2O) is made of two hydrogen atoms joined to an oxygen atom. Carbon dioxide (CO_2) is two oxygen atoms joined to a carbon atom. A sugar molecule ($C_{12}H_{22}O_{11}$) is twelve carbon, twenty-two hydrogen and eleven oxygen atoms all joined together in a special way. The formula of a compound tells us the number of atoms in one molecule of the compound.

Heffernan, A. and Learmonth, S., *The World of Science*, Book Two, p. 65

In order to come to an understanding of this text, we need to look both beyond it to its textual environment and to look within it to its textual features.

THE TEXTUAL ENVIRONMENT

It is a common practice in secondary schools to ask students to read or copy excerpts from textbooks. But to take an excerpt out if its broader context makes it difficult to make useful connections. We need to consider how the environment of the text contributes to an understanding of its meaning. This environment could be envisaged as a number of layers surrounding the text.

At the broadest level we might want to see the text in relation to a number of other relevant texts. We might refer to this as the intertextual environment. At another level, we could locate the text in question within the context of the textbook itself. Science textbooks often contain a number of units, each treating a certain topic. These units consist of related chapters and within each chapter we find a number of different genres.

Let us take a look at each of the layers surrounding our sample excerpt.

The Intertextual Environment

As mentioned previously, the textbook in a classroom does not have an independent existence. It participates in the life of the classroom in conjunction with a number of other texts, including the teacher's explanations of its content, the students' discussion as they refer

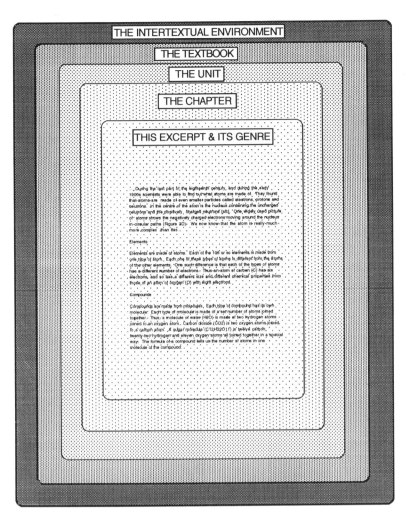

to its instructions for an experiment, the notes scribbled in its margins, other reference books treating similar topics and other volumes in the series of textbooks.

At the pragmatic level of the classroom, the students might be made aware of the variety of resources available to them to help develop scientific understandings and how these complement each other. In particular, the role of the textbook might be discussed so that students are mindful of how they might best utilise what it offers. This might seem an obvious statement to make, but there are students who see the textbook either as being the sole authority and their only source of information, or as having an extremely marginalised status — an alien artefact to be referred to as a last resort.

Beyond the classroom, the book enters into wider cultural discourses concerning such issues as the nature of scientific knowledge and the purpose of schooling. A student's understanding of the book will be an outcome of the interaction of all these texts and discourses.

At this broader level, students might be encouraged to examine the nature of science and the limitations of the textbook in terms of how it mediates scientific knowledge. The teacher might introduce the notion of critical literacy by looking at how science represents a particular (Western technological) way of looking at the world. What part does the textbook play in endorsing this world view? Does it uncritically reproduce this perception of how the world works, or does it attempt to challenge the scientific enterprise in any way? How might other texts and other cultures explain our world? To what extent does the textbook distort the scientific endeavour by presenting it in a simplistic and unproblematic fashion? How might other texts treat topics covered in the textbook? What about issues of human fallibility and scientific fraud disclosed in current newspaper and magazine articles? Where is there evidence in the textbook of the debates, the uncertainties, the frustration and exhilaration of the scientific world?

The Textbook Itself

Just as primary school children are often taught 'book-handling skills', so the secondary student needs to be able to understand how textbooks function as a whole. What areas of science have the authors decided to include? What are the names of the units and chapters? How do they relate to one another? Some textbooks begin with a chapter on the nature of science and its various sub-branches. In the textbook from which our excerpt was taken, the student needs to infer this from the unit headings:

Unit 1:   Astronomy

Unit 2:   Chemical Substances

Unit 3:   Heat and Air

Unit 4:   Cells and Plants

Unit 5:   Looking into Rocks

Unit 6:   Ecology

Also of interest might be such aspects as when the book was written (are certain parts now out of date?); the country of publication (does it constantly refer to unfamiliar contexts?); whether there is a glossary; and the adequacy of the index. Teachers might even need to draw students' attention to features such as the inside of the front and back cover, where commonly used tables are often located for easy reference.

Again, teachers might assume that such basic skills can be taken for granted. But many students coming from primary school have not previously encountered a textbook and unless 'walked through' one, often don't know how to access information for themselves or might not venture beyond those parts of the book specifically designated by the teacher for study. If we want students to become independent learners, then we need ensure that they are able to confidently make their way around the textbook and exploit its accessibility.

The Unit

In science textbooks we usually find a number of chapters that cluster around a particular topic. The sample excerpt comes from the second unit, Chemical Substances, which consists of three chapters:

Chapter 3:   Chemical Groups

Chapter 4:   Elements

Chapter 5:   A Study of Mixtures

As we will see, the understandings about the topic are generally developed throughout the unit of chapters, so the practice of dipping into a chapter and reading a text in isolation from the rest of the unit ignores the authors' careful building up towards greater complexity. In order to easily grasp the notion of elements and mixtures, for example, the student needs to have read the prior chapter on the different chemical groups, where basic concepts and terminology have been introduced.

At this level, students need to develop skills of skimming and scanning a text — to recognise what constitutes a 'meaningful chunk' (in this case, the unit); to skim the text in order to get a general idea of what it's about and to scan the text to locate specific information (using headings, subheadings, topic sentences and other organisational devices).

The Chapter

The structure of chapters in secondary science textbooks is often deliberately predictable in order to facilitate the students' reading. Some books even include a section explaining the organisation of chapters so that students are able to see the significance of each part of the chapter and to locate it easily. This again might seem obvious to the mature reader, but students often are not encouraged to read, or even skim, whole chapters and do not become familiar with the variety of genres or sub-genres within a chapter. Here the term 'genre' is being used to refer to any text used for a particular purpose. In *The World of Science* by Heffernan and Learmonth, a typical chapter would contain:

- A statement of **student objectives** that summarise the main understandings to be developed in the chapter.

- A number of **reports** providing information on various aspects of the topic being treated.

- **Procedural** genres outlining appropriate experiments inserted at relevant points throughout the chapter.

- **Explanations** of a variety of phenomena.

- **Revision questions** at the end of each major section of the chapter.

- A historical **recount** outlining how a particular discovery came about or detailing the development of a theory over a period of time.

- **Biographies** of scientists involved in the area in question.

- The occasional **exposition**, stimulating argument about issues such as pollution and extinction of species.

In this book, the various genres are differentiated by the use of subheadings, outlined boxes and different coloured texts — black for the main content and blue for more peripheral texts. But even with such assistance, it cannot be assumed that students will automatically recognise how a chapter is organised, the roles of the various genres within the chapter, and how these genres relate to one another.

Each genre represents a particular aspect of scientific inquiry. In identifying and discussing the purpose of each genre, students might come to a fuller understanding of the various ways in which scientists explore the world.

The Genre

Each particular genre within the chapter has its own characteristic structure and language features. The experimental procedures, for example, begin with a statement of the **goal** of the experiment.

How can a compound have properties different from the elements used to make it?

This is generally followed by a series of sequenced **steps** telling you what to do. In this case the instructions are followed by a **prompt** to guide observation:

1. *Mix a small amount of powdered iron* (ferrum reductum) *with about twice as much sulphur powder. What effect does a bar magnet, wrapped in clear plastic, have on this mixture?*

2. *Remix the iron and sulphur, and place in a crucible (Figure 3.9). What changes do you see as you heat the mixture over a hot Bunsen flame?*

3. *After allowing the crucible to cool for a few minutes, turn it upside down and tap*

gently. Repeat the magnet test with the new substance. Can you separate the iron and sulphur with the magnet?

4. *Does the new substance have different properties compared to iron and sulphur?*

There are also optional elements such as **cautions**: Try to keep clear of any of the gas given off. Often there are **diagrams** illustrating certain steps in the procedure.

With a report, we generally find some sort of **opening generalisation**, often in the form of a definition: **Compounds** are pure substances that can be split up by chemical means. This is followed by a **description** of the phenomenon in question, with the information organised in particular ways. In scientific reports, this information is frequently organised in terms of taxonomies showing how different phenomena are related to each other in a systematic way. One type of taxonomy is that of a whole/part relationship, where scientists try to describe what the world is composed of. We find evidence of such a taxonomy in the sample excerpt.

*. . . atoms **are made of** even smaller particles called electrons, protons and neutrons.*

*. . . the nucleus **containing** the uncharged neutrons and the positively charged neutrons [sic].*

*Elements **are made of** atoms.*

*Compounds **are made of** molecules.*

*Each type of molecule **is made of** a set number of atoms joined together.*

A whole/part taxonomy that we could infer from the above quotations might be represented like this:

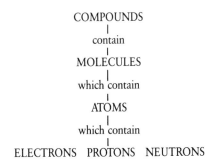

A WHOLE/PART TAXONOMY

Another way in which information is organised in scientific reports is through a classification taxonomy. This is where scientists describe the world in terms of groups and subgroups, on the basis of particular characteristics. This type of taxonomy is at the heart of an understanding of chemical substances. But in order to infer this taxonomy from the text, we need to read the whole unit on Chemical Substances. Spanning these three chapters we find a 'macro-genre' describing chemical substances and their relationship to one another. When we examine these chapters carefully, we can come up with a taxonomy indicating different types of chemical substances:

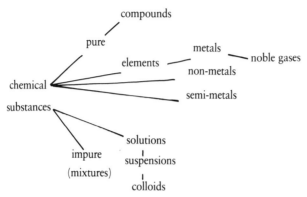

A CLASSIFICATION TAXONOMY

If we seek to induct students into scientific ways of construing the world then (among other things) they need to understand the nature of taxonomies. Few texts make these taxonomies explicit in diagrammatic form. It is up to students to recognise them from
the texts in which they are embedded. When the taxonomies are spread over a number of chapters and when each chapter consists of a number of genres interrupting the flow of the taxonomy, it is essential that students receive assistance in accessing this information from the text.

One way that teachers could guide students to identify these patterns in the text is by jointly constructing diagrams such as 'A classification taxonomy'.

Another important consideration at this level is teaching the students how to read the various types of diagrams and charts that accompany the various genres. Explanations in particular are often represented in relatively complex diagrams and flow charts. It is difficult to fully understand the explanation without an understanding of the diagram. Again, such skills cannot be taken for granted.

INTO THE TEXT

Let us return to our sample excerpt. We have looked at the environment of this text and pointed out how our understanding of it is influenced by the surrounding text and co-texts. Now let's explore the excerpt itself and try to identify those features that could cause difficulties for the novice reader. There are several language features that are characteristic of the written language found in science textbooks. Here we are only going to examine two features — technicality and abstraction.

Technicality

Each subject area explores how the world works in its own distinctive way. These different ways of construing the world are reflected in the language of the discipline. At the most basic level this can be seen in the specialist terminology that has evolved to meet the needs of each of these areas. Many regard this terminology as unnecessary jargon that simply confuses students. It is important, however, to realise the function of technical terms. They are used by scientists to refer to aspects of their field in ways that are unambiguous and convey exactly the same meaning to anyone else working in the field. This is crucial in a displicine that depends so much on such notions as reliability, precision and replicability. Attaching commonly understood labels to shared understandings is also an efficient way of operating. It means that the technical term can be used as a form of shorthand between colleagues, avoiding the necessity of having to constantly explain a concept or process.

If we are serious about inducting students into the discipline of science, then they need to be comfortable with the language of science. They need access to this language (and to the concepts behind the language) in order to participate in the discourse of science. A science textbook cannot therefore avoid the use of technical terms. The dilemma for textbook writers and teachers is how to introduce this terminology without alienating the students. Most well-written junior science textbooks would approach a topic from an everyday perspective, helping the students to identify with the ideas involved. The concept in question would be developed in familiar language as much as possible, perhaps accompanied by hands-on activities and oral exploration. The students would then be moved on to the less 'commonsense' notions and into the more 'scientific' ways of conceiving of the world. At this point the scientific terminology comes into play. When a term is first introduced, it is printed in bold letters to indicate that a definition can be found at this point. To consolidate the understanding, a number of examples are often given. For example:

> **Compounds** *are pure substances which can be split up by chemical means. This is because compounds are made of two or more elements chemically joined together.* Water *contains hydrogen and oxygen.* Carbon dioxide *contains carbon and oxygen.* Sugar *contains the elements carbon, hydrogen and oxygen chemically joined together.*
>
> *The World of Science* p. 57

Introduced in this way, technical terms need not be seen as a source of difficulty in reading a scientific text. In fact for students of non-English-speaking background in particular, the technical terminology presents fewer problems than everyday words with less precisely defined meanings.

Abstraction

In addition to the technicality encountered in science textbooks, the level of abstraction in these texts is likely to cause problems in reading for many students. Much scientific knowledge is of an abstract nature — and this is increasingly the case as students move through secondary school.

One grammatical resource characteristic of scientific abstraction is **nominalisation**. This refers to the common practice in science of changing a 'process' into a 'thing' (or an abstraction). In the chapter on Elements, for example, the properties of metals are expressed in more process terms using verbs:

1. How well can the metal conduct electricity?

2. How well can the metal conduct heat?

3. How easily can the metal be hammered or flattened into sheets?

4. How easily can the metal be drawn into wires?

5. Does the metal break when you try to bend it?

6. Does the surface of the metal look dull, glassy or metallic?

7. What are the metal's melting and boiling points?

In scientific text, these processes are generally turned into abstract 'things' (or nouns), such as conductivity, malleability, ductility, and so on.

This has the effect of summing up the process and enabling the text to move on. Having described the process of how a metal and the gases in the air react together, we can from then on refer to this process using the noun, 'corrosion'. This can be illustrated in an excerpt from Chapter 4, Elements, in *The World of Science*.

> *The chemical activity of a metal helps determine how it is separated from its ore. There are two main methods:*
>
> *1. The less active metals are **extracted** in a blast furnace, for example, iron, lead.*
>
> *2. The more active metals are **extracted** using electricity, for example, aluminium, sodium.*
>
> *We can do both of these **extractions** in the laboratory.*

The processes ('extracted') have now become a thing ('extractions').

Once a process has become a 'thing', it is able to enter into relationships with other things. This facilitates the scientific endeavour of trying to identify relationships within the world. A scientist is able, for example, to describe the relative degrees of malleability, reactivity, resistance and conductivity of one metal as apposed to another, without going into long-winded explanations each time of the various properties.

Even at the junior secondary level, textbooks abound with nominalisations. In the chapter from *The World of Science* on Elements, for example, we constantly come across nominalisations such as the following:

- the activity series
- its ease of extraction
- natural sources
- the rate of corrosion
- good conductors of heat
- chemical reactions
- these extractions

Compared with a senior secondary science text, however, the junior texts are extremely considerate of their readers. The abstraction and compactness of senior texts makes huge demands on the reader. In just two years, the readers of our sample text will be faced with the following in their senior text:

> The **measured conductivity** of very pure forms of the carbon allotropes graphite and diamond indicate that carbon is the best **thermal conductor** of all the elements. The **conductivity** of these solids is very sensitive to **impurities** and trace amounts can cause marked **reduction** in **conductivity**.
>
> Wiecek, C. *Chemistry for Senior Students*, p. 19

In oral language, we tend to 'unpack' the nominalisations (in bold) by changing them back into their verbal form. For example, we might have said something like:

> If we take very pure forms of graphite and diamond, which are carbon allotropes, and measure how well they conduct heat, we would find that carbon is able to conduct heat the best of all the elements. These solids are very sensitive to impurities. Even a tiny amount of an impurity can greatly reduce how well they are able to conduct heat.

Students who have not been exposed to nominalisations through sustained reading of scientific texts, will most likely find the highly nominalised prose of senior textbooks quite daunting. While some authors overuse nominalisation when they could have written in a more reader-friendly way, it is nevertheless an integral and functional part of scientific prose and cannot be completely avoided. Students need to become accustomed to both reading nominalised text and using nominalisations in their own writing. Teachers aware of this potential difficulty (and some uses of nominalisation are more likely to cause trouble than others), can draw the students' attention to such forms as they read and can 'unpack' the nominalisations if necessary (or ask the students to unpack them, perhaps by retelling the sentence or text in the way they would say it orally).

CONCLUSION

As we have seen, teachers cannot assume that students coming from primary school automatically know how to read secondary science texts. They need to constantly support the students in their reading of these texts in a variety of ways.

Firstly, they need to be able to evaluate textbooks and select an appropriate one for their students — one that uses language in a considerate way to clarify rather than obfuscate, and yet one that also does not patronise the readers by avoiding the sort of language that is necessary to appreciate how scientists operate.

Secondly, teachers need to encourage the regular use of the textbook, so that students regard it as an integral part of classroom practice. This means reading to find out information, reading to review and consolidate topics and concepts introduced orally, reading to find out how to do things, such as experiments, reading in groups, reading with the teacher, reading to oneself and reading at home with parents.

Thirdly, teachers need to help students develop understandings about how these texts work at the various levels outlined above and the strategies they might need in order to process such texts effectively. This becomes increasingly the case as students move through secondary school. Senior texts are generally highly abstract, dense, technical, grammatically complex and make a lot of demands on the reader. Students need to be initiated into such language over a long period of time.

Finally, teachers need to support students in their reading of the texts — from providing preliminary experience so that students build up sufficient understanding of the topic before reading the text, to reading the text together and guiding them to recognise and deal with potential difficulties at the level of the whole text through to specific grammatical points. Used effectively, textbooks should empower learners by making them independent. In order for this to happen, however, students need to know how to read them.

References

Heffernan, D.A. and Learmonth, M.S. (1980), *The World of Science*, Book Two, Longman Cheshire, Melbourne.

Wiecek, C. (1989), *Chemistry for Senior Students*, Brooks Waterloo, Melbourne.

Jo Coffey

When I was at school science was learnt from books. There was one book for every year level, with drawings of apparatus and a few photographs. At the end of every chapter there were test questions. The teacher used these questions to make sure you had read the chapter and learned all the science. I did not like my science book very much, but I always felt that I really liked science and all the things that the word meant to me. I would also have liked to explore other things that were not in the book, such as astronomy. As we did not, however, study certain topics in school science, we found books to learn about what we wanted to know.

For example, at home we had a bird book that my family bought soon after our arrival in Australia. It was quite a difficult book to read as the author used a special shorthand which gave large amounts of information — if you understood the language used. We were very intrigued by all the new birds we saw in our garden and so quickly learned to read the strange abbreviations. I still have *An Australian Bird Book*, and I help children to use it every year in my classroom. I think of it as a *real* science book, and in using it I have come to understand what an important part books play in science learning.

USING BOOKS IN THE SCIENCE CLASSROOM

Children should be encouraged to use many different books to learn about science. A book can be the expert to refer to for an answer or clarification, or a book can spark an interest or an investigation. More often, however, books simply serve to deepen a child's understanding of some familiar topic, helping them to make increasing sense of the wor'd and function more confidently in it.

In most schools now, it is possible to have a wide range of books in the classroom at any one time. Most school librarians encourage bulk borrowing to enhance silent reading time and provide material for literature and thematic studies. Municipal libraries also lend freely to local schools and teachers can include non-fiction titles with a science focus in any bulk borrow selection.

Reading programs provide another source of books and most of these now include science topics. In the last few years an excellent range of science 'big books' and accompanying small books have been produced. As with the reading programs, these books come with teacher resource books suggesting how best to use them.

I augment these resources with books and magazines from my own collection, mostly bought cheaply at fetes, book sales and through children's book clubs. I also add my old treasures, such as Leach's *An Australian Bird Book* so creating an enviable class library — and a science resource I can use in many ways.

THE INCIDENTAL LEARNING OF SCIENCE

One of the great advantages of a large collection of science books is being able to capitalise on events as they happen, so satisfying the immediate needs of children for scientific information. Sometimes it is only a simple question that needs to be answered in order for a child to be able to talk or write confidently about a topic.

Morning talk and news time can become more satisfying and valuable when children have the opportunity to use books to assist their presentation. For example, children who bring unidentified insects in bug catchers and jars enjoy identifying them in books. Most insect books are fascinating, and they also help to promote careful observation and meaningful discussion. While the search for the specimen is on a wealth of general information can also be gleaned about insects and spiders. When I direct children to these books, I allow them to take their time searching for the relevant information. I watch them learning incidently as they discuss the features of a variety of creatures, while still engrossed in their own specific searches.

Children who are seeking the identification of something by looking in a book are very involved in the scientific process. They must look closely at their specimen and decide on its particular characteristics. This observing and classifying goes on until they decide that they have found what they are looking for in the book. This equates with the hypothesis, which is then explained and tested through the presentation to the class.

The role of the teacher is to encourage these processes and allow the necessary time for them to occur. When Iona broke her arm, I asked her if she knew which bone it was. She had forgotten, but felt she might recognise the name of the bone if she heard it. As a class we listed the possible bones it could be. This resulted in a considerable list of bones, some possible and some more suited to a verse of "Dem Bones, 'Dem Bones'.

Iona and a friend then looked through some books to find the name of her broken bone. As a teacher, I had the choice of encouraging a private investigation or involving the whole class. I could develop the interest into a unit of study, or let it pass as an incidental science activity, depending on the curriculum outline I had chosen for the year.

The science questions that need immediate answers often occur in the context of writing. When Mark said, 'I need to know how tall Great Danes grow for my pet story,' he expected to find the answer in a book. When Ahmed wrote about the wind in Libya he knew it had a special name. He could not remember it and started searching until he found the sirocco mentioned in a book about the weather.

There are a wealth of other opportunities for science learning that occur incidently. Some do not require recourse to a book. An active investigation might be a more appropriate way to answer a question raised, as might a discussion. Books can, however, offer credibility and authentication when it is needed, particularly if the topic or focus is outside the ordinary.

When some beautiful sunsets began to occur recently, John's father told him they were due to the eruption of a volcano. The class was collecting and classifying rocks and minerals, and John told us about his father's comment when we talked about igneous rock. Volcanoes intrigue children and the chance comment slotted in perfectly with the science theme. The consequent search for the volcano in question required books, and a different set of books was used to find out how to make erupting volcanoes in the classroom. The children were interested enough to bring other books about volcanoes that they found in the local library, as well as articles cut from newspapers.

Many valid science experiences occur incidentally. By encouraging the use of books, magazines and newspapers that contain science information, the classroom teacher can offer the children opportunities to increase their understandings about their world, and to develop positive attitudes towards seeking and using information.

It is also important that talking and sharing occur when books are in use. The text used in a great many non-fiction books can be difficult and children may lose the meaning. Talk helps the teacher to check understanding and so assist the child to make the connections between the written word and the concept.

Sometimes, however, these concepts elude the child, despite careful explanation and exposure to books and experiences. I subscribe to the Constructivist view that this understanding will develop as one concept builds upon another and sense is made in the child's own time. Many science books written for children can be used for incidental learning, and also as a focus for planned science experiences to help the development of more complex understandings.

PLANNED SCIENCE TOPICS

I try to take advantage of the science books available for children when I plan a unit of work or a theme. I also use reference books written for teachers. These are often full of activities, and I sometimes let the children have access to them as well. There are now a great many teacher resource books in the area of science education that come with books for the children to use. These are a great aid for planning lessons particularly for the generalist teacher who lacks confidence in the area of science. We can learn along with the children, and the format of many of the teacher resource books make them particularly useful for teachers committed to the integration of curriculum.

I like to use these published science programs with teacher's guides and books for children to read, but I also make use of other books. I generally introduce my planned topics before the books, although I am sure there are times when reading a book is an interesting way to begin a science unit of work. It can be better to take a step back before doing this and check on the understandings that the children already have about the subject.

An open-ended question will solicit answers that will guide planning. When I asked the children to name the tools they had at home, they mentioned the predictable ones like spades, hammers and power drills. We listed them all to refer to later. I then knew what they understood by the term 'tools'.

Later we looked back at this list to see what we could add to it. I had avoided the temptation to read a book about tools before we had built up some understandings and tried some activities. I felt it was better to use activities to introduce the concept that tools made certain tasks easier. I wanted the children to use a range of items we generally do not refer to as 'tools' and have them discover the connection. Later, when we read about tools and simple machines, the children's comments showed that both interest and understanding were greater.

When the children look to books at this stage of the process, they can then cope with the wider perspective more likely to be found in a book than in a classroom activity. They also find new ideas to develop that are related to the topic. As a teacher, I then become the resource person, assisting the children in following their own line of inquiry. Time is also provided for them to report back to the class and reflect on their understandings.

The reporting back or explaining process is vital in all curriculum areas and very much part of the scientific process. I encourage children to use language such as, 'I thought this would happen and/but...'; 'I read this...'; 'Now I am going to try this, and I think that this will happen...'. The reporting back can be oral or in a written form. I also expect the children to refer to and show the books they used, giving the book's name and the author.

Children often believe science to be the manipulation of test tubes by men in white coats, with a big bang expected at the end of each experiment. Overcoming this stereotypic view of scientists is an exciting unit of work to do with children.

I start by asking, 'What is Science?' We list all the words and statements that are suggested and discuss them to see if we can group them in any way. Sometimes children suggest groupings such as 'Space' and 'Chemistry', and I happily accept any suggestions.

Then I ask, 'What science do you do at home?' Most children say none, for their perception is often limited and rarely do things from home appear on the first list. When I bring out a large box labelled 'Home Chemistry Set', the children usually wriggle with delight, for they think it *is* going to be test tubes and big bangs. Out of the box I bring some soap, jelly crystals, fly spray, and a few other household products. Perhaps the children are disappointed in what they see, but the idea becomes clear very quickly, and they are soon able to list applications of science in the home.

The children are then free to choose some physics or chemistry that comes from home and prepare an investigation to show the class. There is often great diversity in the presentations, from stain removal through to how to remove labels from ice-cream containers. Many children turn to books at home for inspiration, as topics such as cooking and paper-making are investigated.

A home science display can be arranged as children investigate their topic and record the science concepts they have discovered. The reporting back and the displays allow all children to share the investigations. The teacher's role is simplified to that of school resource person and adviser, as parents assist with this role at home, helping children to organise their investigation and then describe and explain it.

I have also collected a range of children's science experiment books that they enjoy and find easy to use. These are available to the children for borrowing at any time. Some of the titles are very appealing and include, *What Happens If?*, *Isn't That Amazing!*, *Boiling Water in a Paper Cup* and *How to Make Square Eggs*.

Apart from having the books available for browsing, silent reading and borrowing,

I occasionally present them as an activity-centred unit. In small groups, the children have to find some science activities for the rest of the class. I simply make sure they have the resources for the activity and that they can use the books successfully. I find the children use the science language from the books and are keen to explain the concepts they have learned to other children. Some teachers may prefer to limit the activities or the number of books available for use in a unit like this. Either way, I find it encourages children to try the experiments in the books, which they otherwise are content to simply read.

SPECIAL INTERESTS AND HOBBIES

Many people have special science interests and abilities. My mother grows very unusual African violets, and one of my brothers shares my fascination with astronomy. I know children who know more about rocks, turtles or telescopes than many adults. As a teacher, I feel it is important to nurture these interests and encourage the sharing of this special knowledge. In most cases, it is this sharing that inspires a similar interest in another person.

For example, the Museum of Victoria recognises the wonderful collections that children sometimes have. A colleague's daughter was able to proudly display her remarkable collection of 256 toy rabbits. The rabbits may not have been science, strictly speaking, but the collecting and classifying process which was undertaken certainly was.

I endeavour to borrow books about the particular interests of any child, and I try to encourage them to share their enthusiasm with others. We held a museum in our classroom where everyone displayed either their collection, or the oldest thing they could find. Each exhibit had to have a label and a card explaining its significance. This required a diversity of books to research, in order to provide an explanation that was clear and concise. The label on all the old things had to make reference to the concept of 'change'. For all the collections, the labels showed how they could be classified or sorted.

It was clear that the children were intrigued by one another's collections, and the diversity of old things was amazing. There was a trilobite fossil, an old bottle with a marble seal and a fine silk fan from China. Each of these objects was researched using books and its special significance examined. Different understandings of the science concept of change were able to be discussed in relation to each exhibit, as well as many other individually significant features.

Capitalising on the expertise of the children and of significant adults can make a science program relevant and interesting. It is also possible to build on interests that are not altogether scientific, but which allow us to diverge towards areas of science. James, for example, loves anything to do with Tibet. After he wrote about the country and showed his research books, we tested our powers of extra-sensory perception and compared our lives for a week with what the astrologers had predicted. I helped James plan some activities by referring him to certain books.

Books play an important part in my classroom in all curriculum areas. This does not mean, however, that we are locked into passive, book-centred learning. We use books in a variety of ways. I sometimes outrage people by writing in the margins of my books and underlining relevant passages in order to help children use them. I am also careful to explain to children that these are my books and that I do this for a purpose. I would like children to collect some useful books of their own and keep them and use them all their life, as I do with my *An Australian Bird Book*.

Science books are often simply enjoyable to read and should be used for that purpose alone. We also need them, however, to answer the questions that the children's scientific investigations often raise. We need them for information, inspiration and clarification.

I reiterate my belief that these scientific activities, although they involve books, encompass all the processes that are central to science, including describing and observing, classifying, hypothesising, testing, predicting and explaining. Furthermore, they begin with children's present understandings, and foster development from this point through interest and worthwhile activity.

Bibliography

Ardley, N. (1991), *Science For Kids Series*, Little Ark Books, Australia.

Eldin, P. (1979), *Isn't That Amazing!*, Armada, London.

Frauca, H. (1968) *Australian Insect Wonders*, Rigby, Australia.

Leach, J. A. (1942), *An Australian Bird Book*, (8th Edition) Whitcombe and Tomb, Melbourne.

MacCauley, D. (1988), *The Way Things Work*, Readers Digest, Australia.

Mascord, R. (1970), *Australian Spiders in Colour*, Reed Books, Australia.

Meyer, J.S. (1972), *Boiling Water in a Paper Cup*, Scholastic, New York.

Taylor, B. (1990), *Fun With Simple Science*, Kingfisher, London.

Temple, P. and Levinson, R. (1982), *How to Make Square Eggs*, Hamlyn, UK.

Wyler, R. (1975), *What Happens If?*, Scholastic, New York.

ABOUT THE AUTHORS

Johanna (Jo) Scott works in the Department of Language and Literature at Deakin University, Toorak Campus. Before that she taught in Victorian primary schools and was a General Curriculum and Language consultant. Her interest in the relationship between science and language learning led her in 1990 to produce a video, *Language Through Science*. She is currently writing (with Jenny Feely) a series of science investigation books, *Science Starters*, published by Collins Dove. Jo is the Victorian State Representative on the National Council of the Australian Reading Association.

David Keystone is a practising primary teacher at Seaford Primary School, Victoria.

David has displayed a keen interest and has had vast experience in the teaching and learning of science through his own classroom practice and involvement in the delivery of professional development programs.

David has worked as a science consultant for the Victorian Ministry of Education and contributed to the development and dissemination of the Victorian Ministry's *Science Framework* document. He was also a sub-editor for *Investigating: Australian Primary Science Journal* and is the co-author of two teacher resource books, *Cracking Up!* and *Shaping Up!* In 1989, he and his class of students were featured in a video production, *Language Through Science*, produced by Victoria College.

Lyn Turner has had extensive experience as a primary teacher and ESL consultant. In recent years she has also been involved in establishing and supporting a LOTE program. She is currently a lecturer in the Department of Language and Literature at Deakin University, Toorak Campus.

Jenny Feely is an experienced classroom teacher who has taught at all levels of the primary school. She has a great interest in the teaching of science and the links between science and language development.

Jenny has published two books, *Science at Play* and *Mission Possible*, both of which provide classroom teachers with practical ideas for implementing science in their classroom. She is currently working on another book, *Science Starters*.

During 1992 Jenny will be teaching at Meadow Heights Primary School.

Lesley Wing Jan is a classroom teacher at Eltham East Primary School, where she currently teaches Grade Six.

Lesley is interested in the process of professional development and teacher change. Her current research relates to how children learn to spell, the structures and support needed to help children develop as competent spellers and their perceptions of the spelling process. Lesley's favourite activities are exploring with children how they learn language, learn through language and learn about language.

Lesley is the author of *Write Ways: Modelling Writing Forms*, OUP, 1991 and *Spelling and Grammar in a Whole Language Classroom*, Ashton Scholastic, 1991.

Nea Stewart-Dore is a freelance literacy consultant. Trained as a secondary teacher, Nea has, however, taught at all levels of schooling. Most recently she was Senior Lecturer (Literacy Studies) at the former Brisbane CAE. Her main interests lie in collaborating with classroom teachers to develop strategies for enhancing students' literacy learning in school subjects, and in advising on the design and implementation of teacher development programs.

A foundation member of the ARA, Nea has served on National Council and is currently convener of the Literacy and Learning in Secondary Schools Special Interest group.

Beverly Derewianka is currently Senior Lecturer in Language Education at the University of Wollongong, having previously taught at primary and secondary schools and in TAFE.

Beverly's major research area is the language development of children in the transition to adolescence, hence her interest in the difficulties some children have in reading and using textbooks as they enter secondary school. In particular, she is concerned with how students of non-English speaking background cope with the language demands of both primary and secondary school.

Jo Coffey learns with the children at Middle Park Primary School.

Jo loves classroom teaching at any primary level, because it offers such diverse opportunities for learning in an interesting and exciting way. Her other major interest is promoting the partnership of parents and teachers in the learning process. She is an EMIC (Exploring Mathematics in Classrooms) Tutor, and is involved in the Family Maths, Family Science, Families Count and Towards Real Independence programs.

Her classroom reflects her commitment to integrating learning based on children's needs and interests, and she enjoys planning for this with the children and the team of enthusiastic teachers at her school.